# Rigby INFOQUEST

Grade 6

# TEACHER'S RESOURCE

# Contents

**Student Books Overview and Notes** . . . . . . . . . . . . . . . . . . . . . . 36

# About *Rigby InfoQuest*

*Rigby InfoQuest* is a nonfiction series of resources for enhancing literacy development and learning across your class's curriculum. Current research and curriculum developments have highlighted the need for students to develop visual literacy and critical thinking skills in addition to the decoding and text processing skills associated with learning to read. It is becoming increasingly important for students to become self-directed learners who can logically research and then coherently present information. *Rigby InfoQuest's* rich components provide many opportunities for introducing these crucial skills, inviting engaged practice, and encouraging students' extension of their learning.

## This Teacher's Resource

On the following pages you will find ideas and activities for guiding your students' reading of the nonfiction materials in the series so they will also have a better understanding of other nonfiction texts and visuals that they need to use in the world. The suggestions provide a variety of ways that you can flexibly best support your students' learning based on their needs. Included in this Teacher's Resource are blackline masters for comprehension practice and assessment.

## InfoMagazines

There are 2 InfoMagazines for each grade level 5 and 6. These engage students as you introduce nonfiction organization or features, demonstrate skill use, and share curriculum content in a group or whole-class setting. You will find helpful, specific suggestions for using the InfoMagazines in this Teacher's Resource on pages 28–35.

The InfoMagazines can be used for a variety of purposes, including introducing students to the special content features, text organizers, and visual literacy elements they will meet in the Student Books.

Each InfoMagazine offers a range of possible teaching points. Suggestions for informal assessment of each of these teaching points are included in the InfoMagazine notes. The outcomes of the informal assessment can be used to help select Student Books that feature elements to be taught, consolidated, or further explored. (See the Student Book Overview on pp. 36–39.) The InfoMagazine notes also include 2 blackline masters that encourage critical thinking skills.

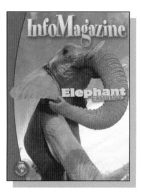

## Student Books

There are 20 different Student Books for each grade level 3–6 catering to ages 8–11. Each grade is color coded: grade 3 is orange, grade 4 is green, grade 5 is blue, and grade 6 is purple. The books supplement each grade's curriculum and content area requirements. These Student Books contain:

- manageable main text leveled for the age group's average reading ability.
- text organizers, including tables of content, headings, subheadings, bullets, captions, labels, indexes, glossaries, and bibliographies.
- visual elements so students interpret diagrams, cutaways, cross sections, maps, keys, tables, graphs, charts, and time lines.

Please see pages 36–119 of this Teacher's Resource for book-specific suggestions.

## www.rigbyinfoquest.com

Each Student Book has its own specially designed Web site pages, with text leveled to match the Student Book. Two activities are provided on the Web site for each Student Book.

# Using the *Rigby InfoQuest* Web Site

Your students will log on to the secure "Siteseeing" Web site at **www.rigbyinfoquest.com** to delve further into a topic from each Student Book. They can find information to answer research questions, which are provided for you on pages 41–117 of this Teacher's Resource, and they can also complete extension activities. The site can be ideal for classroom use or homework.

## Teacher Registration

It is best to go to **www.rigbyinfoquest.com** using the *Internet Explorer* browser. This site uses Flash software; an onscreen prompt will identify if your computer has the correct software or not. If your computer does not have it, simply follow the hyperlink to freely download Flash.

Set up an individual user name for each student. To allocate these user names, click the "Teacher Log In" button. This brings up a screen on which you can create and maintain a class list. [Note: As you fill in the fields, there is a space for your ZIP code. You must fill this in. If you do not have a ZIP code, insert any number so you can continue. If you are uncertain about what to do at any point, the Help button can provide information.]

Follow the registration process. Click the "Register" button and type in the fields. When you have completed all the fields, click the "Register" button at the bottom of the page. You will be directed to a student registration page. Here, enter each student's name and grade level of work. This will automatically generate a user name for each student.

| Student List | | |
| --- | --- | --- |
| **Student** | **User Name** | **Grade/Year** |
| Charlotte Michaels | CharlotteM | Grade 6 |
| Dylan Smith | DylanS | Grade 6 |
| Mike Egmont | MikeE | Grade 6 |
| Samantha Duffy | SamanthaD | Grade 6 |
| Tara Ryan | TaraR | Grade 6 |

Click here for a version of the student list you can print

The grade that is selected for students will determine whether they access the Grade 3, 4, 5, or 6 section of the Web site when they log in with their user names. The information you enter will be displayed as a printable list.

## Student Log In

A student logging in simply goes to **www.rigbyinfoquest.com**, clicks the "Student Log In" button, and enters her or his user name in the provided field. The Siteseeing main page will next appear so the student can begin work.

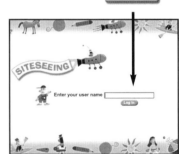

## Site Navigation

From the Siteseeing main page, a user navigates to any of the topic areas by using the zone icon buttons. When a zone is clicked, a list of topic areas appears; the appropriate topic area that corresponds with the banner on page 3 of the Student Book currently being read can be selected.

What do you call a group of elephants? Visit **www.rigbyinfoquest.com** for more about THE ANIMAL KINGDOM.

- A student navigates through the reading pages of the selected topic area and logs out by using the clickable bar located in the top right corner of each page. If there is ever a problem loading a complete page, the page button in the bar can be clicked to refresh the content.

- Red text signifies that a box with additional information is available. Blue text signifies that a dictionary definition is available. The student clicks on the text to link to the information.

- When the cursor is moved over an image and the symbol changes from an arrow to a hand, it signifies that an information box is available from the image. The student clicks anywhere on the image to link to the information.

The activities for a topic area can be accessed from Page 4. The "Click here" button brings an activity onscreen. Writing activities can be completed onscreen, and all activities can be printed when they are completed.

When any activity has been completed, the student should click the "Log out" button to record that the activity is completed. This will record on the class list that the student has completed an activity for the Student Book.

Students can navigate to a different zone at any time. They can do this from all the topic areas by clicking one of the banner icons along the left side of any reading page.

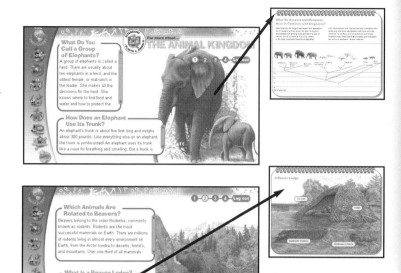

**ARROWS TO SCROLL THROUGH TEXT**

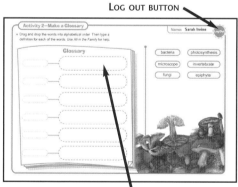

**KEYBOARD PRINTING INSTRUCTIONS**

**LOG OUT BUTTON**

**TEXT CAN BE TYPED ONSCREEN**

**BANNER ICONS**

# Special Content Features

Every book in *Rigby InfoQuest* contains several special features to extend or challenge students' reading and thinking about extra information. At the Grade 6 level, these are…

### Interesting information about the origins and meanings of words

Word Builders can be used to broaden vocabulary and the understanding of how words work.

### Questions directly related to text and illustrations

Students can search text and illustrations for specific information.

### Detailed, behind-the-scenes close-ups

This information takes students deeper into topics but is not more complex text.

### Interesting historical facts

Time Link can lead students to consider what they are learning in a broader context.

### Tips and fascinating facts about inventions and development

Students can relate what they are reading to real-life applications.

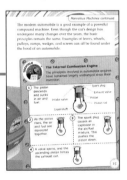

### Biographical information

Famous people, their careers, and their achievements over challenges are the focus.

### Newspaper reports, interviews, and magazine articles

Students are encouraged to connect what they are studying with what is happening in the world.

## Snippets of useful, intriguing information

These facts increase general knowledge and can be the basis of further research.

## Information related to environmental issues

Earth Watch can help students focus on contemporary environmental issues.

## Presentation of both sides of an issue

Students are given the opportunity to form and justify opinions about a range of issues.

## Narrative text in a diary format

Students can read personal diary entries written by a variety of people.

## Procedural text

Students are given opportunities to read and follow sets of instructions and create anything from a mold terrarium to a time capsule.

## Information, research ideas, and interesting activities

Students explore this safe Web site to build research skills, learn, and demonstrate their learning for assessment or evaluation.

## Research Starters
### Challenging Questions

Research Starters can be used before reading a book to introduce topics, encourage research, and access students' interest and prior knowledge, or they can be used after reading the book to generate further research and discussions.

# Nonfiction Text in the Classroom

## Considering Genre Differences

Nonfiction text differs from fictional material in significant ways.

- Nonfiction text has more text organizers, more visual literacy elements, and often a variety of genre.
- Usually, nonfiction material does not need to be read from front to back.
- Perhaps the most important difference is that the learning outcome goals that are planned for reading nonfiction material are quite different from those for fictional material.

## Choosing Learning Outcomes

The learning outcomes planned for fictional text often focus on the process of reading. For example, goals may be set so students build their abilities to

- monitor their own reading.
- use appropriate reading strategies.
- self-correct when meaning breaks down.
- read with fluency and expression.
- comprehend a story.

While the learning outcome goals for nonfiction text certainly include these reading process skills, there are critical thinking skills that are highly important for successful comprehension of nonfiction material. These include:

- recognizing important information
- forming generalizations
- evaluating fact and opinion
- comparing and contrasting
- sequencing and summarizing
- classifying, categorizing, and organizing
- interpreting maps and diagrams
- judging validity of information
- identifying cause, effect, and consequences.

In general, it is the ability to use these critical thinking skills that students need to develop as they move from *learning to read* to *reading to learn*.

## Thinking About Readability

The perception of students' reading materials needing to be at specific reading levels sometimes precludes teachers from using nonfiction in their literacy teaching. They may be unsure of texts' reading levels. The readability level of any text is influenced by a range of factors.

### The Readers's Background Knowledge

What readers bring to a text strongly influences their abilities to comprehend it. To some extent, teachers can build background knowledge before students read texts.

**The Vocabulary**

Simple words don't necessarily make a book easier to read. In nonfiction texts, the glossary can be used to familiarize students with unfamiliar and technical vocabulary.

**The Text Structure and Sentence Complexity**

The way information is organized, presented, and illustrated is an important consideration in making texts accessible to young readers. Teachers can help students by teaching about characteristics of common organization in nonfiction texts such as headings, subheadings, labels, captions, body copy, contents, indexes, and glossaries.

**The Cohesiveness and Coherence of the Text**

When selecting nonfiction texts, consider what the text requires of each reader and what the reader brings to the text. The factors that influence readability levels of nonfiction texts can be manipulated by the teacher, thus making a wide range of books accessible for the majority of the class.

The body copy of the books and Web site in the *Rigby InfoQuest* series is at the average grade level (Grade Three, age 8 years; Grade Four, age 9 years; Grade Five, age 10 years; Grade Six, age 11 years). Each grade's texts have been trialed with the age group for which they are intended. They are suited for a guided reading approach with most students in an age group, resulting in students' 90–95% accuracy when reading the text. The special content features in the books usually contain more challenging text. These may require a shared or reading aloud approach.

## Planning for Success

The following steps are useful for planning the reading of nonfiction material.

1. **Decide what the learning outcome(s) will be for the reading.**
   Based on the needs of the students and the content of the selected text, choose one or more learning outcomes for students to achieve.

2. **Set purpose(s) for reading.**
   Before the reading, you will clarify with your students what the purposes are and what they will learn.

3. **If you will be guiding students' reading, plan questions and activities.**
   These questions and activities will support students to achieve the learning outcomes.

4. **Plan how you or students will model responses to the text and visual elements.**
   The modeling will demonstrate how to use information related to the learning outcomes, and the information can be recorded using an appropriate format.

5. **Prepare for responding and appropriately extending learning.**
   Students may complete what has been modeled and use what has been learned in different ways.

6. **Decide how you or students will assess their reading and thinking.**
   Assessment should be focused on the learning outcomes.

# Using *Rigby InfoQuest*

## Choosing Texts

To broaden understanding of topics, genre, text organizers, and visual elements, there are choices for comprehensive reading experiences. The overviews on pages 36–39 will help you to quickly locate related books for your choice.

1. The whole or part of an InfoMagazine may be initially read or later reread to introduce, clarify, or extend what is met in a Student Book or other curriculum studies. Then more Student Books with related content can be read.

2. Select books around a general topic. Work through these, using the appropriate teaching approach with groups of students or your whole class.

3. Groups of students at the same or different reading levels may wish to form interest groups, select books to read, and then discuss what they've read for curriculum related or recreational reading purposes. The main role for you is to help the students select appropriate material and then ensure the students who need support are receiving it, either from you or from other students. Remember the Web site offers research questions that broaden book topics and suggests other connected Student Book reading.

## Choosing Approaches to the Texts

There are flexible ways you can use the texts with your students and teach with this resource. Your knowledge of the needs and capabilities of the students and the requirements of the curriculum will help determine which approaches will be appropriate.

There will be times when it is important for the whole class to gain specific content from a particular text. You can make any book in *Rigby InfoQuest* a successful reading experience for all students by altering the teaching approach.

The choosing of an approach is the major way of controlling text difficulty. Whether working with an individual student, a small group, or the whole class, you can choose one or a combination of the approaches.

- For the first reading of an InfoMagazine and with students who may find a Student Book's text overly challenging, the approach can be a combination of *reading aloud* and *shared reading*.
- With students reading slightly below the level of a text, *shared* and *guided reading* can be used.
- With students reading at or slightly above the level of a text, the approach can be *guided* and some *independent reading*.
- For students reading well above the level of a text, you may choose to set research questions and have the students read the text *independently*.

## Reading Aloud

When passages of text are overly challenging for students, the first reading can be one of your reading to them. This enables students to concentrate on the meaning of the passages. A conversation about the text should be shared before and following the reading. The discussion will support and help develop the students' fuller understanding of the text.

## Shared Reading

You may wish to highlight information that is unfamiliar to students. Reading these passages with your students enables you to focus on specific detail while maintaining student involvement. It is often useful to use oral cloze, withdrawing your voice on words or phrases that students can manage or when you wish to observe the students' attempts. As in reading aloud, there is also a conversation about the text.

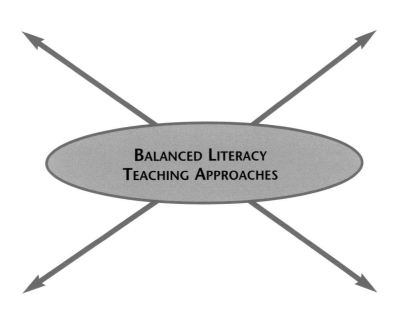

BALANCED LITERACY
TEACHING APPROACHES

## Guided Reading

When text material is at an appropriate level of challenge, you can preview and ask questions to guide students' focus on their reading. As students read silently, you can observe the strategies they are using to process the text and understand the information. Support is given individually when it is required. It is important during previewing and questioning to use the vocabulary that students will meet in the text.

## Paired and Independent Reading

You may wish to combine more capable students with those needing support. Although this needs to be carefully monitored, there are often benefits for both students. Questions can be posed that focus the students' research reading. When the text to be read is well within students' capabilities, a passage, a page, or even the whole text can be assigned to be read independently.

# Tips for Teaching Text Organizers

Text organizers abound in informational text, and students need to understand them to be successful readers and writers. The following are suggestions for procedures that can be applied to many texts.

### Tables of Contents

- Turn to a contents page. Discuss the placement of text and page numbers. Have students practice quickly turning to an appropriate page. For example, using the *People of the Past* Student Book, ask *Can you find the section about the rise of city-states? Which comes first—"A Place in Time" or "Cave Life"?*
- Discuss the author's decision to arrange the text in the order seen on the contents page. Ask questions such as *Why do you think the section "Cave Life" is at the front of the book? Why is "Contributing to the Future" near the end?* In general, help students understand the logical arrangement of the contents page and how it can be used to quickly find main headings.

### Indexes

- Turn to an index. Show students that the entries are arranged in alphabetical order. Explain the conventions of page numbering such as single pages separated by commas and multiple, consecutive pages indicated by a dash.
- Have students practice using the index to find specific information. For example, *Turn to any page that mentions farming. Show me the main section about weapons.*

### Glossaries

- Have students skim a book's text and list all the words in the body, excluding headings, that are in boldfaced type. Then have them write those words in alphabetical order. Turn to the glossary and ask *What do you notice?* (The words and order should be the same.)
- Read through glossary entries with students. Then challenge students to suggest why these specific words have been chosen for inclusion. Ensure everyone understands that glossaries contain only words that are directly related to the book's subject.

### Bibliographies

- Turn to page 31 of *Peace Makers*. Show the students the "Bibliography" section, and together read the entries. Can students explain that a bibliography is a list of materials the author used to find information for writing the book?
- Highlight that the entries are in alphabetical order. Discuss the other conventions used: author's surname first; title in italicized type next; the name of the publisher; and finally, the year of publishing. Show students how to conduct a library search using these entries.

### Headings

- Turn to any main section of a Student Book and read the heading to students. Ask *What information would you expect to find on this page?* Talk about how authors try to compose headings that clearly indicate what will be included in the body text.
- Turn to another main section and use a self-adhesive notepaper to cover the heading. Read the page to students and then have them brainstorm appropriate headings. Unmask the heading and discuss it in the context of the students' choices.

## Subheadings

Turn to a page such as page 28 in *Our Inside Story* with the heading "Spare Parts." Show students how the author could have chosen to use subheadings (perhaps "Prostheses" and "Cosmetics" in this example) to present the information in another logical and clear way.

## Labels

- Turn to a page featuring labels, such as page 9 in *Monuments and Mummies*. Point to the labels and show students that the accompanying body text often refers to these labels. Turn to another example, such as pages 10 and 11 in *Giants of the Deep*, and have students read the labels. Then have students search for text that refers to each label.
- Discuss how a label helps readers clarify their understandings of the related text.

## Captions

Choose a page with captioned text. Discuss how the text in the caption(s) is about the image, and the two together present a more complete picture. For example, on pages 6 and 7 of *All in the Family*, have students read and discuss the relationship between the captions and the diagram. Challenge them to think about other ways the author could have organized the text (plain text, bulleted points, etc.).

## Bullets

Turn to a page containing bullets—page 15 of *On the Move*, for example. Show students how using bullets is a way of highlighting and summarizing information. Then choose suitable pages without bullets (like pages 18 and 19 of *On the Move*), and help students rewrite the text in bulleted format.

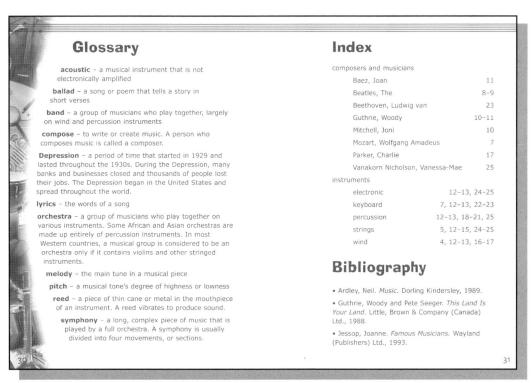

EXAMPLE OF THE GLOSSARY, INDEX, AND BIBLIOGRAPHY FROM *MUSIC, MUSIC, MUSIC!*

## Tips for Developing Visual Literacy

There are many visual elements throughout the series to reflect the many that students will need to use well in the world. The main focus of teaching to develop visual literacy is to help students use these elements so they can gain optimum meaning and ultimately be able to produce similar elements. Being visually literate, students can better demonstrate understanding, record information, and communicate.

### Photographs and Illustrations

- Read a page heading to the students, and then cover the rest of the text. Have the students carefully study the illustration. Invite them to articulate all the information they gain from the illustration alone. Then uncover the text and have students read it. Ask *How did seeing the illustration help you read the text?*
- Have the students look at combinations of visual elements and text. For example, using pages 10–11 of *Giants of the Deep*, say *What are the humpback whales doing? What is important about the illustrations involving the plankton and krill?* Discuss the students' responses and then read the text on these pages. Discuss how the combination of illustrations help in understanding the text.
- Turn to a page featuring a photograph. Discuss the differences in composition between photographs and illustrations. Help the students understand why an author would choose to use one instead of the other (detail required, photo opportunity, and so on).

### Diagrams

- Ask about a diagram *How do we read it? Where do we start? Can we start in different places?* Write the text from the diagram on a chart, and read through it with students. Compare the chart with the diagram to lead into a discussion about how having both the text and diagram helps a reader achieve a better understanding.
- Lead students in comparing and contrasting a variety of diagrams. A few you might focus on are on page 7 of *Shifting Perspectives*, pages 22–23 of *The Weather Engine*, page 15 of *Close Up on Careers*, and page 18 of *The Invisible World*. Can students generalize that a diagram is a visual made to clearly show what something is, how it works, or the relation between parts?

### Maps and Keys

- Discuss different kinds of keys—ones with letters, numbers, colors, symbols, and patterns. Then work with a map and accompanying key, such as on page 5 of *The Weather Engine* or page 8 of *Tides of Change*. Demonstrate and have students practice using the key to find a specific fact from the map. Help students understand that this can be an efficient and comprehensive way of presenting certain types of information.
- Students can compose their own maps of the school or neighborhood, complete with keys.

### Cutaways

- Turn to a cutaway and carefully look at the illustration. Talk about how without cutaways, there would need to be two separate illustrations, and the effect would be lost.
- Turn to page 24 of *On the Move*. Ask students how the cutaway section helps them better understand the inside of an automobile.

## Cross Sections

- Locate a suitable cross section, for example, on page 12 of *Digging for History*. Explain how this visual is similar to a cutaway but often much more expansive and designed to show an entire picture from both the outside and inside.
- Demonstrate how cross sections usually include text and sometimes include keys or arrows indicating movement.

## Tables

- Choose a page containing a table, for example, on page 29 of *Giants of the Deep*. Help students understand that tables are a useful way of displaying numerical information (weight, height, sports information, and so on).
- Students can take a simple survey such as about eye and hair color and compose a table of results.

## Charts

- Locate one or more charts in the Student Books, for example, on page 8 of *On the Move*. Help students understand that charts are used as a way of presenting text material, much the same way that tables are used to present numerical data.
- Read through a chart, making sure that students understand how a lot of information can be simply displayed in this format.

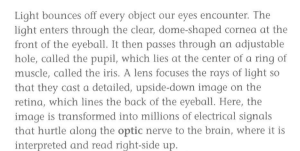

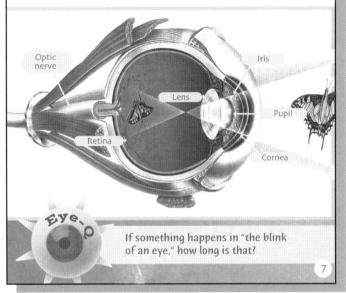

Light bounces off every object our eyes encounter. The light enters through the clear, dome-shaped cornea at the front of the eyeball. It then passes through an adjustable hole, called the pupil, which lies at the center of a ring of muscle, called the iris. A lens focuses the rays of light so that they cast a detailed, upside-down image on the retina, which lines the back of the eyeball. Here, the image is transformed into millions of electrical signals that hurtle along the **optic** nerve to the brain, where it is interpreted and read right-side up.

Eye-Q

If something happens in "the blink of an eye," how long is that?

7

**EXAMPLE OF A CROSS SECTION FROM *SHIFTING PERSPECTIVES***

## Graphs

- Choose a page displaying a graph. Page 20 of *Cogs in the Wheel* has a pictograph, for example. Discuss the way pictures are used as an aid to understanding the graph. Then have students practice finding and interpreting information from the graph.
- Review other types of graphs the students may be familiar with, including line and pie graphs. Discuss when the use of these might be appropriate, and then have students compose bar, line, and pie graphs for a set of provided or gathered facts to see which graph best portrays the data.

## Time Lines

- Select a time line. You might choose the one on page 29 of *People of the Past*. Point out that the dates and events are arranged in chronological order. Help students understand that making a time line is a good way to visually display a rate of change or to memorialize important events.
- Students can compose time lines featuring important events in their lives.

# Sparking Discussions and Research

## Research Reading

To a large extent, the ultimate goal of any worthwhile literacy program is to have the students able to recognize their own needs and work independently in achieving their own goals. In the early stages of independence, it will be important to select appropriate research questions for individual students. It is equally important to model and review discovered examples of different ways the results of research can be communicated.

Each of the Student Book teaching notes, pp. 40–119, has a list of suggested research questions for independent readers, and the "Research Starters" in each Student Book is also a good source. The www.rigbyinfoquest.com information included in each Student Book's teaching notes also provides research questions that are answered on the Web site.

When your students become more independent with reporting and researching results in a variety of ways, you may want to have them set their own research questions and make their own decisions about how to display and report their findings.

## Using the Research Starters

The "Research Starters" page at the end of each Student Book can be used in different ways, either before reading or after reading the book.

## Choices Before Reading

- Choose one of the four research starters and invite groups of students to brainstorm what they already know. The group can next research further and report back. You can then combine all the groups' findings into a major list. This can either be added to as the book is read or amended after the book has been read.
- Assign a different research starter to pairs or small groups of students. After their research, have them report back to the large group. Then have the large group suggest other possible answers and useful sources for research.
- Choose a research starter; have students search the contents page and the index for page references they think will help them acquire information to answer the question.
- Choose a research starter for groups of students to research and present their findings in the form of a debate.

## Choices After Reading

- The activities above will also be appropriate after the book has been read.
- Choose one research starter and have students review their reading of the text and visuals to gather information.
- Assign different research starters to small groups of students. Have the students list all the new information they gained to answer as a result of having read the text. Each research starter and list can then be shared with the rest of the class and expanded.
- Have students choose a research starter to research possible answers, perhaps as a homework activity.
- When students have explored one or more of the research starters, have them generate a list of further questions they can research.

## Suggestions for Using the Web Site

Each Student Book contains a reference to Siteseeing on the www.rigbyinfoquest.com Web site. The site is a source of extra information about a specific topic and two learning activities for each book, all thematically connected to students' reading. Please see the Student Book Overview, pp. 36–39 of this resource, for a complete listing of the on-site topics.

When students have read a Student Book and go to its accompanying Web pages, they will find the first three pages have a question-and-answer format. There are up to six questions included. These questions are listed for your reference in the teaching notes for each book on pp. 40–119.

When appropriate, students can access the site as a homework activity. They can be assigned to research and complete one or both activities. Alternatively, individual or groups of students could be given questions to research within the classroom setting and then present the results in different ways. All the activities can be printed. If the students are working at home, you will need to ensure that they have their user name and that they know the address of the site.

You can assign and encourage students to present their understanding of information using a range of formats. Presentations may include written questions and answers, newspaper or magazine-style articles, interviews, visual or electronic displays, and oral presentations.

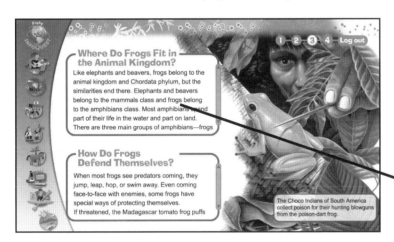

> Important—Remember to
> close each information box
> before proceeding.

# Extending with Special Content Features

Considering students' needs, valuable extensions of their learning, and your curriculum, you can make the most of the special content features in each Student Book of *Rigby InfoQuest*. Besides using Research Starters and the Web Siteseeing connection, these activities are suggested as general guidelines for the other features.

## Word Builder

- Have students use a dictionary to generate more words from word parts.
- Use the target word to find more words with their origins in other languages.
- Begin to compose a glossary of new words.
- Begin a chart that includes new words, their origins, and other related words or synonyms and antonyms.
- When appropriate, use the words in Word Builder as a source of spelling words to learn or topics to write about.

## Fast Facts

- Have students read the Fast Facts question on the "Features" page and respond to it before reading the Fast Facts.
- Begin a list of interesting Fast Facts, so the students can continue to add to it and use the list as a classroom source in later research or writing.
- Use the Fast Facts to help generate research questions.

## Try This!

- Have students follow the instructions and complete the activity.
- Use the Try This! format to help students generate their own procedural text.
- Begin a class file (perhaps of hobbies, recipes, and so on) of written procedural text that the students can refer to for ideas.
- Set up a Try This! area in your classroom. Permission is given by the publisher to photocopy the Try This! activities for this purpose. Paste an activity onto a card, and put it with the required materials in the Try This! area. The students might even take the Try This! cards home for homework activities.

## Techtalk

- Use the terms in Techtalk to begin a class glossary of technical terms.
- Generate research questions based on the information contained in Techtalk.
- Have students write about how a particular piece of technology affects them personally.

## In Focus

- Because of text complexity, the In Focus features may best be approached by reading to or sharing the reading with students. As you explore these features together, discuss why the In Focus was included in a particular section and its relevance to the topic.
- Help students recognize the main point(s) of an In Focus. Then write and jumble the main points to have students place them in the correct sequence.
- Have students generate and investigate research questions from these features.
- Demonstrate and then have students rewrite an In Focus text in another form, such as bulleted or outline.

## In the News

- Highlight the format of news articles, including headlines, dates and places, bylines, paragraphs, and photographs.
- Have students search local newspapers for related information.
- Use a topic of interest to begin a class newspaper.
- Use a particular news article to generate a range of research questions.

## Profile

- Because of text complexity, the Profile features may best be read to the students or by sharing the reading. In discussion, you can help students understand biographical format such as chronology, key dates, main points, and so on.
- Use the Profile feature to generate research questions.
- Have students use the format of Profile to write their own personal biographical sketches.
- Begin and add to a file of interesting people from the past. This could be arranged in chronological order.

## Time Link

- Use the text of Time Link to demonstrate writing a time line.
- When appropriate, have students use an atlas, globe, or map to find the highlighted area.
- Use the Time Link feature to generate questions for students' research.
- Begin and add to a file of interesting facts from the past.

## What's Your Opinion?

- Have students read the "for" and "against" arguments and justify responses.
- Groups of students could be encouraged to debate the issues.
- Have students write supporting statements for a position.

## My Diary

- Use My Diary to demonstrate chronological writing.
- Use the information to generate research questions.
- Rewrite My Diary information in the form of a report.

## Fact Finder

- Use the Fact Finder to generate research questions.
- Have students compose their own Fact Finder questions.

## Earth Watch

- Have students form and justify opinions on specific issues.
- Students can research environmental issues that most interest them or apply to your area.
- Begin and add to a file of environmental issues.

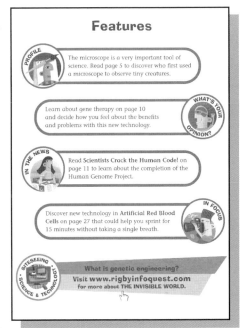

EXAMPLE OF SPECIAL CONTENT FEATURES FROM *THE INVISIBLE WORLD*

# Assessing and Evaluating

The belief that well-constructed learning activities are opportunities for authentic assessment is the guiding principle for assessment and evaluation throughout these resources. Activities for authentic assessment in *Rigby InfoQuest*

- are themselves valuable learning activities.
- occur throughout and after the reading of a text, and are a natural consequence of what has been read.
- provide immediate and ongoing feedback about learning to students and teachers.

Assessment concentrates on the students' abilities to understand and use the text and literary elements of nonfiction material. There are many opportunities for assessing the understanding and use of these highly important skills:

- recognizing important information
- forming generalizations
- evaluating facts and opinions
- comparing and contrasting
- sequencing and summarizing
- classifying and categorizing
- interpreting visual elements
- using text organizers

## Provided Assessment Activities

For each Student Book, assessment tools for use during and after reading are provided in the Student Book Notes of this resource, pp. 40–119.

## During Reading

The "Guiding Learning" section of each book's notes highlights key text and visual elements to discuss. Each of the activities can be assessed informally as the reading progresses, and the results will be a quick indicator of students' learning.

## After Reading

Thinking Activity—For students' practice as well as assessment following each Student Book, a Thinking Activity blackline master involves the use of a key skill or skills. The completed worksheets will provide an ongoing record of students' progress in the main aspects of learning associated with nonfiction text.

Formal Assessment—Each Student Book's Nonfiction Assessment Record is a blackline master for taking more formal assessment. The Assessment Record is derived from the learning outcomes, purposes for reading, and critical thinking skills that can be your teaching focuses for the book. You may use all the sections to comprehensively assess student learning, or you may be selective and choose to assess fewer skills if that is appropriate for an individual student.

**Optional Assessment and Evaluation Activities**

As well as assessing students' abilities to understand and use the elements of nonfiction material, you may also wish to assess the way students use semantic, syntactic, and graphophonic information as they read. Cloze procedures can be used to find out the reading process skills and strategies that students are using.

Cloze procedures can be used with individual students whenever you feel the need for further assessment. You can either use self-adhesive strips on the selected text in a Student Book or photocopy short sections of text and blacken out the appropriate words.

Delete some function words (pronouns, conjunctions, prepositions, and adjectives) to check students' use of syntactic information.

⟶

Some artifacts are easy to find _____ they are above ground. Many, however, are buried _____ the surface _____ Earth or hidden deep _____ overgrown jungles. Some are even lying beneath _____ sea in shipwrecks _____ ancient times.

Delete some content words (nouns and verbs) to check students' use of semantic information.

⟶

Some artifacts are easy to _____ because they are above _____. Many, however, are _____ beneath the surface of _____ or hidden deep in overgrown jungles. Some are even lying beneath the _____ in shipwrecks from ancient _____.

# An Example of Planning and Use

The following is the extended lesson planning of one teacher. She has used the Student Book Notes provided for *Digging for History,* considered the needs of a group of her students, and clarified her lesson goals by using the previously suggested 6-step planning for success model. This plan could be adapted and used with any of the titles in *Rigby InfoQuest.* The bolded sections are items that appear on the assessment master provided in the Notes for the book and show how the teacher plans to incorporate them into the group reading session before later individual assessment. The teacher has added explanations for some of her thinking.

## 1. Learning Outcomes

I want my students to successfully:

- be able to state why it is important to understand the past.
- display an understanding of why temples were important to the Mayans.
- recall ways that archaeologists discover new sites.

## 2. Purposes for Reading

The students need to know that the purposes for them reading the text are:

- to learn how paleontologists discover and date dinosaur fossils.
- to learn the steps undertaken by archaeologists at a dig site.
- to learn about the rise and fall of the Mayan civilization.
- to form and justify opinions about the fate of artifacts from the *Titanic.*

[Note: Appropriate purposes for the particular students have been chosen from both the "Purposes for Reading" and "Critical Thinking" possibilities listed in the Student Book Notes.]

## 3. Guiding the Reading

[This plan for reading the book may be spread out over several sessions, depending on our time available. I will use a mixture of approaches during the reading.]

### Before Reading

- Assign pairs of students Research Starter Number 2 on page 32 of *Digging for History.* Provide time following their discussions for sharing their ideas with the group.
- Give the students time to look through *Digging for History.* Invite one student to find the contents page. Discuss its function. Locate the index and glossary, and discuss the functions they have. Read the words from the index and glossary to the students, and explain that these are words they'll be meeting in the text and learning to use.
- Tell students this book is all about discovering the past. Help students recall their previous studies of ancient civilizations. Ask, *How do we find out about these civilizations? How do people know where to look?* Record the students' responses to these questions. Continue adding and amending responses during the reading.

## During Reading

[I'll remember to use vocabulary that is in the text as much as possible when asking questions to guide students' learning.]

- Pages 4–5: Discuss the illustrations and photographs on pages 4 and 5. I can ask *What is archaeology?* Have students respond and discuss their ideas. Then read these pages to students. Talk about the bolded words. Invite students to use the glossary to find the meanings of "preserved" and "epigraphs."

- **Discuss the importance of studying the past**. Invite students to find and read the specific text that states why studying the past is important.

- Pages 6–9: Have students read pages 6 and 7. Ask, *How do archaeologists know where to look for artifacts?* If students need more support, share read sections of the text. **Then discuss the use of historical record, local stories, and technology in the search for artifacts**. Share read pages 8 and 9. **Discuss the steps taken at a digging site**. Ask, *Why do archaeologists take such great care of the environment while working at a dig site?*

- Pages 10–11: Discuss the nature and format of biographies. Highlight the use of birth and death dates and then the chronological setting of key information. Share read the body text on these pages. Ask, *Why was Mary Leakey's discovery very important?* Then ask, *What qualities do you think successful archaeologists need?* Have students discuss their responses and read the appropriate text on page 11.

- Pages 12–13: Ask, *What do paleontologists do?* Have students offer their ideas and then read the body text on these pages. **Discuss the role of paleontologists**. Read the "Dinosaur Dating" text to students. Help them understand the two main ways of dating dinosaur fossils.

- Pages 14–19: Read page 14 to students. Ask, *How do you think people were able to discover and explore the wreck?* Open the gatefold (pages 15–18) and allow time for students to view the underwater scene. Then have students read these pages independently. Ask, *What is similar and different about the work of underwater archaeologists and the work of archaeologists on land?* Help students read and understand the "In Focus" feature. Read page 19 to students. **Then encourage students to form and justify opinions about the fate of the artifacts from the *Titanic*.**

- Pages 20–25: Point out the time line that runs along the bottom of these pages. Then say, *Read to the end of page 25 to find out who the Mayans were, how they lived, and what became of them.* (Share read with students needing support.) When students have finished, discuss the importance of temples in the Mayan culture. Invite students to use the illustration on page 22 to write their own math equations. Reread page 24 with students. **Discuss the fact that disease, not warfare, was the main reason for the decline of the Mayans.**

- Pages 26–27: Tell students that the text on these pages outlines an amazing discovery made in Peru. Say, *Read to the end of page 27. Find out what was discovered and who helped make the discovery.* When students have finished, discuss the incredible discoveries and how the local people helped.

- Pages 28-29: Ask, *How will future generations find out what life was like during the present time?* Have students respond to the question and then read independently to the end of page 29. Discuss the "Try This!" advice for making a time capsule.

## 4. Modeling Responses

- Remind students that they are going to be composing and recording personal information that they would put into a time capsule. [Thinking Activity Master 5 will be used.]
- Using a copy of the Thinking Activity Master, show students how to fill in the activity sheet. I'll demonstrate what I would include in a personal time capsule. Ensure students are clear about the requirements before having them proceed.

## 5. Responding and Extending

- Distribute individual copies of the activity worksheet and have students complete the exercise.
- When students have finished, we'll discuss the process involved. Have students compare and discuss their responses under each of the six headings. Discuss the reasons why some of the students' responses have differed.

[The following activities are my options for broadening and strengthening the learning outcomes and purposes for reading.]

### Using the Index

Turn to the index. Remind that entries are in alphabetical order. Review the conventions of page numbering such as single pages separated by commas and multiple, consecutive pages indicated by a dash. Have students practice using the index to find specific facts.

### Using the Features Page

Look at the headings and read these together. Have the students find the answers by turning to the relevant pages. They could work individually or in pairs.

### Using the Web Site

- Pose questions to the students. [These are listed in the Student Book Notes.]
  1. How do archaeologists dig up the truth?
  2. How can archaeology help solve a mystery?
  3. What happened to the Anasazi?
  4. Where can dinosaur fossils be found?
  5. How did dinosaur fossils form?

- Make a list of the students' ideas. Explain that the answers to these questions can be found on the Siteseeing Web site. If necessary, demonstrate how to access the site, the zone (Science & Technology) and the link (Archaeology).

- Provide time for the students to research these ideas independently or in pairs and then complete the activities. This may be done at school or at home.

# 6. Assessment

- Make copies of the Nonfiction Assessment Record (page 59) to use individually with each student. [The activities on the assessment sheet are directly linked to the learning outcomes, purposes for reading, and critical thinking skills for *Digging for History*. I will choose to either use the entire assessment sheet or highlight the specific areas I wish to assess for each student.]

- Depending on my observations during the reading and this assessment, I may also use cloze procedures and running records to assess some students' reading process skills.

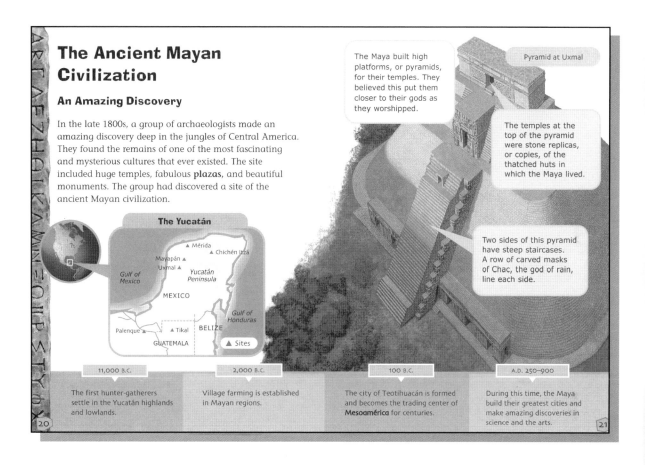

## The Ancient Mayan Civilization

### An Amazing Discovery

In the late 1800s, a group of archaeologists made an amazing discovery deep in the jungles of Central America. They found the remains of one of the most fascinating and mysterious cultures that ever existed. The site included huge temples, fabulous **plazas**, and beautiful monuments. The group had discovered a site of the ancient Mayan civilization.

**The Yucatán**

- ▲ Mérida
- Mayapán ▲     ▲ Chichén Itzá
- Uxmal ▲   *Yucatán Peninsula*
- Gulf of Mexico
- MEXICO
- Gulf of Honduras
- Palenque ▲   ▲ Tikal   BELIZE
- GUATEMALA     ▲ Sites

The Maya built high platforms, or pyramids, for their temples. They believed this put them closer to their gods as they worshipped.

Pyramid at Uxmal

The temples at the top of the pyramid were stone replicas, or copies, of the thatched huts in which the Maya lived.

Two sides of this pyramid have steep staircases. A row of carved masks of Chac, the god of rain, line each side.

| 11,000 B.C. | 2,000 B.C. | 100 B.C. | A.D. 250–900 |
|---|---|---|---|
| The first hunter-gatherers settle in the Yucatán highlands and lowlands. | Village farming is established in Mayan regions. | The city of Teotihuacán is formed and becomes the trading center of **Mesoamérica** for centuries. | During this time, the Maya build their greatest cities and make amazing discoveries in science and the arts. |

20                                                                                          21

# InfoMagazine Notes—*Elephant Exclusive*

## Synopsis
*Elephant Exclusive* explores the fascinating world of elephants. The text highlights the ways elephants communicate, use their trunks, and keep cool. This InfoMagazine includes a look at an elephant orphanage and information about elephant conservation.

## Possible Teaching Points
The following teaching points can be selected for introductions or revisits to nonfiction text, skills, and organizers.
1. Comparing Text Information
2. Summarizing Text Information
3. Reading a Newspaper Article
4. Understanding the Interview Format
5. Reading Persuasive Text
6. Forming and Justifying Opinions
Each of these teaching points can be assessed informally during the reading.

## Visual Elements
Opportunities exist throughout the text to explore the following visual elements.
- a variety of illustrations and photographs
- cartoon elements
- brochure format
- a map with a key

## Special Features
Opportunities exist to introduce or extend cross-curricular learning.
- "In Focus" explores how some elephants mine their own salt.
- "In the News" explains how even elephants sometimes have problems parenting.
- "Earth Watch" highlights the problem of elephant poaching.
- "What's Your Opinion?" lets you have your say on managing elephants.

## Reading the InfoMagazine
### Before Reading
Hand out copies of InfoMagazine Master A. Discuss the activity and have students begin to fill in the KWL chart. Students should continue to fill in these columns as they read the book.

### Sharing the Text
Although the following suggestions involve your reading aloud and shared reading, more capable students can be given guide questions and read independently. (See pages 12–13.)

### *Comparing Text Information*
**Pages 2–5:** Have students look at pages 2 and 3. Discuss the layout and the different kinds of information students expect to find throughout the InfoMagazine. Then share read pages 4 and 5. Challenge students to discuss some of the differences between African and Asian elephants.

**Informal Assessment:** Have students rewrite the "Spot the Differences" information, either in point form or in the form of a comparison chart.

## Summarizing Text Information

**Pages 6–9:** Share read pages 6 and 7. Highlight the way the author has used a combination of body text and text in boxes to summarize facts about elephants. Then share read pages 8 and 9; discuss some of the ways elephants are important.

**Informal Assessment:** Have students reread page 8 and write a statement or two summarizing the main points.

## Reading a Newspaper Article

**Pages 10–11:** Share read these pages and discuss some of the relationships within elephant families. Reread the newspaper article with students, highlighting the format and narrative style.

**Informal Assessment:** Have students reread the newspaper article and discuss some of the ways the format differs from pure expository text.

## Understanding the Interview Format

**Pages 12–13:** Share read these pages. Discuss the way that the type font and captioned snapshots complement the information in the interview. Reread the interview. Highlight the question-and-answer format. Talk about how the interviewer may have developed the questions.

**Informal Assessment:** Have students talk about some advantages of the interview format. Challenge them to say how else the information could have been written. (report form; newspaper article)

## Reading Persuasive Text

**Pages 14–19:** Share read pages 14 through 18. Help students locate examples of similarities between elephants and humans. Then read through the brochure on page 19. Discuss the format and the purpose (to persuade) of this form of writing.

**Informal Assessment:** Challenge students to rewrite part of the brochure as pure expository text.

## Forming and Justifying Opinions

**Pages 20–21:** Read the top of page 20 to students, and discuss the problems facing elephants. Then have students read through the news article and "What's Your Opinion?" sections on pages 20–21, discussing the issues involved.

**Informal Assessment:** Challenge students to form and justify an opinion on the ivory trade or the rights of farmers to kill or capture elephants.

### After Reading

Give students the opportunity to engage in the activity on pages 22 and 23.

# InfoMagazine Master A
### KWL Chart: Summarizing Information

Have students share what they have recorded on their KWL charts before and during the reading. Then have them complete the final column. Discuss the range of resources that are available for answering any remaining questions.

# InfoMagazine Master B
### Elephant Glossary: Locating and Organizing Information

Tell students they are going to create their own glossaries about elephants and read through the instructions together. Make time for comparing the results.

# KWL Chart

Name _____     Date _____

Fill in the KWL chart before, during, and after you read *Elephant Exclusive*.

| What I Think I **Know** About Elephants | Was I Right? | What I **Want** to Know About Elephants | What I Have **Learned** About Elephants |
|---|---|---|---|
| | | | |

# Elephant Glossary

Name _____     Date _____

List all the words below in alphabetical order, and then turn to the appropriate pages in *Elephant Exclusive* to find a form of each word. Write your own definition for each word before you look up and record a dictionary's definitions.

| | | |
|---|---|---|
| herbivore (p. 4) | paleontologist (p. 16) | endangered (p. 21) |
| vegetation (p. 4) | predator (p. 6) | hierarchy (p. 10) |
| carnivorous (p. 9) | matriarch (p. 10) | plummet (p. 21) |

| Word | My Definition | Dictionary's Definition |
|---|---|---|
| | | |

### Synopsis

*Wonders of the World* highlights the Seven Wonders of the Ancient World. It explores more modern wonders, both natural and those constructed by people. The text includes an activity that challenges students to locate places on a grid map of the world.

### Possible Teaching Points

The following teaching points can be selected for introductions or revisits to nonfiction text, skills, and organizers.
1. Using the Contents Pages
2. Reading a Map with a Key
3. Forming and Justifying Opinions
4. Forming Generalizations
5. Reading a Brochure
6. Reading Biographical Text

Each of these teaching points can be assessed informally during the reading.

## Visual Elements

Opportunities exist throughout the text to explore the following visual elements.
- a pie graph
- cartoon features
- brochure format
- a map with a key
- a grid map

## Special Features

Opportunities exist to introduce or extend cross-curricular learning.
- "Time Link" highlights some of the wonders of the ancient world.
- Read "In the News" for an account of an ancient firebug.
- Check out "Profile" and discover an amazing 11-year-old codebreaker.
- Read "Word Builder" and find out what the word *mausoleum* means.

## Reading the InfoMagazine

### Before Reading

Challenge students to discuss some of the natural and created wonders of the world. Ask, *Which of these do you think is the most impressive?* Encourage students to articulate and justify their responses.

### Sharing the Text

Although the following suggestions involve your reading aloud and shared reading, more capable students can be given guide questions and read independently. (See pages 12–13.)

### *Using the Contents Pages*

**Pages 2–3:** Invite a comparison of these and other Contents pages that students have encountered. Have students say what type of information they expect to find in each section. Then select individuals to turn to the appropriate sections and check their assumptions.

**Informal Assessment**: Have students practice using the contents pages. Ask questions such as, *On which page would we find information about a wilderness tour?*

### Reading a Map with a Key

**Pages 4–5:** Share read these pages. Then help students use the key and map icons to locate each of the wonders. Challenge students to suggest which of the seven wonders still stands today.

**Informal Assessment:** Have students practice using the key to locate each of the seven wonders on the map.

### Forming and Justifying Opinions

**Pages 6–13:** Share read these pages, pausing to discuss each of the seven ancient wonders. Help students understand why each of these was special.

**Informal Assessment:** Have students select the wonder they believe was most impressive and justify their opinion with reference to the text.

### Forming Generalizations

**Pages 14–15:** Share read these pages. Discuss each of the seven modern wonders as you progress. Encourage students to discuss the reasons the author may have chosen these particular structures.

**Informal Assessment:** Have students reread these pages and state what these wonders have in common. (Generally, they are described by a superlative—the *longest, tallest, largest,* etc.)

### Reading a Brochure

**Pages 16–19:** Share read these pages. Discuss the importance of preserving the past and the work of UNESCO. Then have students reread pages 16 and 17. Help them recognize some of the devices used in this format (persuasive language, personal approach, visuals which impact).

**Informal Assessment:** Have students select and rewrite two paragraphs as expository text and discuss the differences.

### Reading Biographical Text

**Pages 20–21**: Read these pages with students, and discuss some of the problems and solutions surrounding the Mayan ruins. Then reread the "Profile" on page 20. Discuss the meaning of *biographical* and stress the fact that most biographies contain information about the main accomplishments of the featured person.

**Informal Assessment:** Challenge students to locate and list three important points as they reread the "Profile."

### After Reading

Give students the opportunity to engage in the activity on pages 22 and 23. Can they recall the names of the wonders and more facts?

## InfoMagazine Master C
### Late-Breaking News: Recognizing and Summarizing Important Information

Discuss devices used in newspaper reporting: headlines, columns, photographs, key information, and direct quotes. Then read through the activity with the students.

## InfoMagazine Master D
### Wonderful Facts: Locating and Recording Information

Read through the activity instructions with students. When students complete the activity, they can compare their results.

# Late-Breaking News

Name _____     Date _____

1. Think of an exciting headline for an article about a wonder of your choice and write it on the line.

2. Write your article in the two long column boxes. Use the small box at the bottom to draw the photograph you'd like to include.

© 2004 RIGBY—RIGBY INFOQUEST

# Wonderful Facts

Name _____ Date _____

Use the contents pages of *Wonders of the World* to complete the facts.

| Wonder | Location | Why Special | Type of Wonder (Ancient, Modern, or Natural) |
|---|---|---|---|
| Great Wall | China | Largest structure ever built | Modern wonder |
| Pyramids of Giza | | | |
| Grand Canyon | | | |
| Meteor Canyon | | | |
| Hanging Gardens | | | |
| Eiffel Tower | | | |
| Golden Gate Bridge | | | |
| Colossus of Rhodes | | | |
| Great Barrier Reef | | | |

# Student Books—Overview

| Title | Key Content | Learning Outcomes | Critical Thinking | Visual Elements | |
|---|---|---|---|---|---|
| *All in the Family* | classifying living things<br>plant kingdom phyla<br>animal kingdom phyla | names of 5 kingdoms<br>oxygen and carbon cycles<br>why animals live in groups | generalizing about the<br>  animal kingdom<br>summarizing changes in<br>  the dog family<br>classifying/organizing<br>  information | sequential diagrams<br>charts with bulleted points<br>nature cycle diagrams<br>double-page spreads | |
| *Built to Last* | why people built amazing<br>  buildings<br>use of technology<br>progression of building<br>  heights | why the Tower of Pisa leans<br>the Taj Mahal's significance<br>types of architecture in St.<br>  Peter's Church | interpreting a map with<br>  captions<br>forming/justifying opinions<br>  about architectural styles<br>locating/summarizing<br>  information | a map with captions<br>diagrams with labels<br>double-page spreads<br>a bar graph | |
| *Close Up on Careers* | different types of media<br>caring careers<br>famous people<br>the variety of choices | career planning<br>everyday use of computers<br>main categories of scientists | matching job descriptions<br>comparing roles<br>organizing/summarizing<br>  information about careers | cartoon elements<br>labeled illustrations<br>double-page spreads<br>a diagram | |
| *Cogs in the Wheel* | conditions before and<br>  advances during the<br>  Industrial Revolution<br>inventors<br>features of the Second<br>  Industrial Revolution | defining industrial revolution<br>conditions in industrialized<br>  cities<br>the ongoing nature of<br>  revolution | generalizing about events in<br>  America<br>forming/justifying opinions about<br>  child labor<br>using text organizers in a time line | captions<br>pictorial graph<br>illustrations and<br>  photographs with<br>  leadered labels<br>double-page spreads | |
| *Digging for History* | fossil dating<br>steps taken in an<br>  archaeological dig<br>rise and fall of the Mayan<br>  civilization | importance of understanding<br>  the past<br>importance of Mayan temples<br>discovering dig sites | comparing/contrasting<br>  archeologists<br>forming/justifying opinions about<br>  the *Titanic* relics<br>planning a personal time capsule | sequential diagrams<br>a range of maps<br>continuing time line<br>double-page spreads<br>leadered captions | |
| *Escape!* | people who have escaped<br>  danger<br>risking life to help others<br>bibliography | dangers faced by *Apollo 13*<br>difficulties faced by runaway<br>  slaves<br>why dogs are useful in rescue<br>  situations | generalizing about qualities for<br>  surviving disasters<br>forming/justifying opinions about<br>  POW escapes<br>composing an interview | cartoon elements<br>text in a puzzle<br>illustrations and historical<br>  photographs | |
| *Famous Faces* | remembering historical<br>  figures<br>commemorating bravery<br>perceptions of beauty | why some fame lasts<br>effects of media on famous<br>  people<br>contributions of gifted and<br>  talented people | generalizing about Anne Frank's<br>  diary<br>justifying opinions about privacy<br>  rights<br>reporting on a moment of fame | cartoon elements<br>quotes<br>double-page spreads<br>captioned and labeled<br>  content | |
| *Giants of the Deep* | different kinds of whales<br>how sharks are classified<br>creatures of different<br>  ocean layers | natural dangers facing ocean<br>  ships<br>why sharks are successful<br>preservation of ocean habitats | summarizing differences in fish and<br>  cetaceans<br>justifying opinions about whaling<br>locating/matching information<br>  about ocean creatures | diagrams with labels<br>a map with a key<br>labeled illustrations and<br>  photographs<br>a table of data | |
| *Monuments and Mummies* | lives and roles of the<br>  pharaohs<br>ancient Egyptian<br>  monuments<br>steps of mummification<br>ancient writing forms | Nile Valley conditions<br>reasons for pyramid<br>  construction<br>importance of the Rosetta<br>  Stone | comparing/contrasting life in<br>  ancient Egypt<br>generalizing about Egyptian society<br>summarizing information in a chart | a map with labels<br>captioned illustrations and<br>  photographs<br>double-page spreads<br>a variety of diagrams | |
| *Music, Music, Music!* | universality of music<br>different musical styles<br>variety of musical<br>  instruments<br>constructing an index | significance of folk music<br>influence of electronic<br>  instrumentation<br>The Beatles' role in changing<br>  pop music | generalizing about cultural music<br>comparing musical styles<br>summarizing musician information | captioned illustrations<br>scrapbook formatting<br>labeled photographs<br>music notes on staff | |

| Vocabulary Development | Text Types | Comprehension Skill Activity Master | Assessment | Siteseeing www.rigby infoquest.com |
|---|---|---|---|---|
| *amoeba, antibiotic, biome, Carnivora, carnivore, chlorophyll, evolve, herbivore, mammal, mold, phloem, photosynthesis, spores, xylem* | procedural text e-mail format biographical text expository text | Thinking Activity Master 1: classifying, categorizing, and organizing information about living things | function of classification system similarities and differences in living creatures why animals live in groups | Zone: Plants & Animals Link: The Animal Kingdom |
| *architecture, Baroque, Mannerist, mausoleum, obelisk, philosophy, reinforced concrete, Renaissance, stonemason, symmetrical* | brochure format expository text historical perspective | Thinking Activity Master 2: locating and concisely summarizing information as "Did You Know?" answers | reasons why amazing buildings are built finding information on a map architectural styles use of technology in building | Zone: People & Places Link: Buildings |
| *contractor, curator, font, live broadcast, professional, voluntary work* | text in bubbles biographical text procedural text expository text | Thinking Activity Master 3: organizing and summarizing information about a future career | differences in types of media types of scientists common use of computers professions of care | Zone: People & Places Link: Careers |
| *assembly line, crop rotation, developing country, enclosure, industrialization, interchangeable part, lock, mass production, mechanization, patent, pauper apprentice, selective breeding, synthetic, textile* | historical text biographical text expository text | Thinking Activity Master 4: locating, sequencing, and recording information in a time line | natures of the first and second Industrial Revolutions conditions of people in industrialized cities problems faced by developing countries | Zone: Past & Future Link: The Industrial Revolution |
| *analysis, anthropologist, conquistador, epigraph, Mesoamérica, nonperishable, paleontologist, plaza, preserve, radioactive, sedimentary, survey* | procedural text time line expository text biographical text | Thinking Activity Master 5: composing and recording personal information in the form of a time capsule | importance of understanding the past different types of archaeology ways to date fossils aspects of Mayan civilization | Zone: Science & Technology Link: Archaeology |
| *Allies, French Resistance, Gestapo, political oppression, Special Operations Executive, Underground Railroad* | newspaper report mythology speech balloons expository text biographical text | Thinking Activity Master 6: recognizing important information to compose interview questions and possible responses | survival qualities of astronauts aspects of the Underground Railroad reasons for bibliographies | Zone: People & Places Link: Escapes |
| *alias, annex, caricature, celebrity, commemorate, head of state, heritage, Holocaust, icon, immortal, infamous, media, memento, monarch, prodigy* | biographies diary format expository text procedural text speech balloons | Thinking Activity Master 7: composing and summarizing information in the form of a report | how historical figures are remembered differing views of beauty effects of media the right to privacy | Zone: People & Places Link: Famous People |
| *barb, bioluminescence, camouflage, cartilage, dredge, echolocation, fathom, hull, moratorium, overfish, pack ice, prehistoric, sustainable* | newspaper reports historical perspective procedural text expository text | Thinking Activity Master 8: locating and matching information about ocean creatures | dangers facing ocean ships categorizing creatures in ocean layers why sharks are successful how ocean habitats are being preserved | Zone: Plants & Animals Link: Sharks |
| *canopic jars, civilization, demotic script, dynasty, Egyptologist, embalmer, excavation, hieroglyphs, natron, pharaoh, sarcophagi* | historical perspective instructional text expository text procedural text | Thinking Activity Master 9: summarizing information in the form of a KWL chart | reasons for the growth of civilization in Egypt differences between the rich, poor, and pharaohs importance of the Rosetta Stone and pyramids | Zone: Past & Future Link: Ancient Egypt |
| *acoustic, ballad, band, compose, Great Depression, lyrics, orchestra, melody, pitch, reed, symphony* | scrapbook format biographical text expository text bibliography format | Thinking Activity Master 10: organizing and summarizing information gathered about music and musicians | importance of music in different cultures how music styles differ effects of electronics constructing an index | Zone: Art & Entertainment Link: Music |

# Student Books—Overview

| Title | Key Content | Learning Outcomes | Critical Thinking | Visual Elements |
|---|---|---|---|---|
| *On the Move* | different forms of energy ways energy is consumed forces in nature | force and energy relationship potential and kinetic energy nature of simple machines | forming/justifying opinions about power sources sequencing energy transformations locating and matching information | flow diagrams labeled diagrams bulleted points sequential elements a chart |
| *Our Inside Story* | affects of nature and nurture anatomy/physiology advances functions of body systems | determining personal traits components of the nervous system changes in the brain during sleep | summarizing immune system functions forming/justifying opinions about nature versus nurture locating and recording information about body systems | diagrams with leadered labels a game board microscope and x ray images cross sections |
| *Peace Makers* | people working for peace nonviolent approaches to peace development of the Red Cross | significance of the Nobel Peace Prize how ordinary people make a difference important roles of the United Nations | generalizing about peace makers forming/justifying opinions about forms of protest composing, sequencing, and summarizing in a profile | a time line a map with leaders and a key historical photographs cartoon elements a bulleted list |
| *People of the Past* | prehistoric life hunting/gathering to farming life in city-states | where early people lived benefits of trade reasons for city-states | generalizing about control of fire summarizing changes long ago composing information in diary form | sequential diagrams captioned time line bulleted points maps and photographs |
| *Rebels and Revolutions* | revolutions throughout history outcomes of French Revolution nonviolent protest | causes of revolutions why revolutions continue today importance of the Technological Revolution | generalizing about revolutions summarizing facts of the Chinese Revolution locating and organizing information about revolutions | maps with keys/labels captioned world map double-page spreads historical photographs and illustrations |
| *Secrets of the Sky* | development of telescopes main objects in the universe history of space exploration | importance of the sun to life on Earth importance of the Hubble Telescope meteoroid and meteorite differences | summarizing the Big Bang theory forming/justifying opinions about extraterrestrial life summarizing to write information as a newspaper report | sequential diagrams diagrams with labels illustrations with captions a time line space photographs |
| *Shifting Perspectives* | improving eye conditions brain function changing perceptions | difficulties associated with sight Helen Keller's contributions role of perspective | sequencing events forming/justifying opinions about stereotypes organizing a glossary | optical illusions diagrams labels and a key a time line |
| *The Invisible World* | how modern electron microscopes work structure and function of DNA bacteria and viruses | uses of microscopes functions of microchips possible benefits of nanotechnology | forming/justifying opinions about genetic research summarizing forensic techniques sequencing information about a crime scene | sequenced diagrams with captions a cutaway diagram microscope images double-page spreads |
| *The Weather Engine* | factors affecting the weather atmosphere layers high and low pressure systems | the climate zones effects of an El Niño weather condition weather forecasting techniques | interpreting a weather map forming/justifying opinions about global warming gathering, recording, displaying, and analyzing weather information | captioned illustrations maps/diagrams with keys and labels thought bubbles leadered labels directional arrows |
| *Tides of Change* | population growth world trade and transportation changes in technology | meaning in a population map effects of global travel problems associated with fossil fuels | summarizing benefits and problems of alternative fuels generalizing from graph data forming/justifying opinions about global issues | maps and graphs keys sequential diagrams range of photographs and illustrations |

| Vocabulary Development | Text Types | Comprehension Skill Activity Master | Assessment | Siteseeing www.rigby infoquest.com |
|---|---|---|---|---|
| *air resistance, atom, buoyancy, drag, energy, equilibrium, force, kinetic, lubricant, physicist, pulley, streamlined, radiant, resultant, thermodynamics* | biographical text<br>procedural text<br>instructional text<br>expository text | Thinking Activity Master 11: locating and matching information about simple machines | how forces work on objects<br>generating electricity<br>kinetic versus potential energy<br>energy transformation | Zone: Science & Technology<br>Link: Physics |
| *anatomy, blood platelet, cadaver, circulatory system, conscious, cosmetic, diagnosis, dominant, hallucinate, insomnia, neuron, physiology, prosthesis, recessive, skeletal, subconscious, trait* | historical perspective<br>board game text<br>expository text<br>list | Thinking Activity Master 12: locating and recording important information about systems in the body | use of technology in medicine<br>gene function<br>affects of nature and nurture<br>understanding how body systems function | Zone: Science & Technology<br>Link: Illness |
| *boycott, concentration camps, constitution, diplomat, discriminate, ethnic, ghetto, humanitarian, massacre, Nazis, neutral, occupy, oppress, pacifist, political prisoner, prejudice, treaty* | historical text<br>diary format<br>expository text<br>biographical text<br>list | Thinking Activity Master 13: composing, sequencing, and summarizing information in the form of a profile | violent vs. nonviolent protest<br>how the Red Cross helps<br>importance of the United Nations and Nobel Peace Prize<br>contributing to world peace | Zone: People & Places<br>Link: Peace |
| *artifact, carbon, city-state, civilization, domestic, handicraft, historian, ice age, prehistoric, surplus, ziggurat* | historical perspective<br>list<br>expository text | Thinking Activity Master 14: composing, sequencing, and summarizing in diary form | benefits of farming and fire<br>major changes long ago<br>the rise of city-states | Zone: People & Places<br>Link: Prehistoric People |
| *boycott, colonist, Communist Party, democratic, dictatorship, discriminate, equality, frontiersman, liberty, pacifist, segregate* | historical text<br>biographical text<br>diary format<br>expository text | Thinking Activity Master 15: locating and organizing information about a range of revolutions | pre-conditions of revolutions<br>why revolutions and protests continue today<br>nature of technological revolution | Zone: People & Places<br>Link: Revolutions |
| *astronomer, Big Bang theory, black hole, eclipse, electromagnetic spectrum, galaxy, gravity, light-year, nebula, orbit, simulator, universe* | poetic text<br>historical text<br>expository text<br>interview<br>newspaper report | Thinking Activity Master 16: recognizing and summarizing important information in the form of a newspaper article | main objects in universe<br>importance of the sun<br>what Galileo's telescope helped prove<br>importance of the Hubble Telescope | Zone: Science & Technology<br>Link: Outer Space |
| *electromagnetic, illusion, optic, paradox, peripheral, stereotype* | biographical text<br>historical perspective<br>interview<br>expository text | Thinking Activity Master 17: locating, checking, and organizing information in a glossary | how the eye works<br>how perspective can change interpretation<br>differing perceptions | Zone: Plants & Animals<br>Link: Animal Eyes |
| *contaminate, electron, forensic scientist, genome, microorganism, property, protein, replicate, revolutionize, RNA, specimen* | interview<br>biographical text<br>expository text<br>newspaper report<br>bibliography | Thinking Activity Master 18: composing and sequencing information about an imaginary crime case | how microscopes work<br>viruses<br>forensic science<br>functions of microchips<br>the function of DNA | Zone: Science & Technology<br>Link: The Invisible World |
| *altitude, computer modeling system, condense, deflect, evaporate, geostationary, humidity, meteorologist, ozone, ultraviolet radiation, water vapor, windchill factor* | procedural text<br>expository text<br>diary format<br>bibliography | Thinking Activity Master 19: gathering, recording, displaying, and analyzing information about weather | climate zone differences<br>El Niño effects<br>weather in high and low pressure systems<br>weather forecasting<br>effects of global warming | Zone: Water, Earth, & Sky<br>Link: Climate |
| *developed countries, developing countries, general cargo, inorganic, life expectancy, obsolete, reclaim, renewable resources* | opinion<br>report<br>expository text | Thinking Activity Master 20: forming and justifying opinions on six global issues | interpreting maps and graphs<br>benefits of faster global travel<br>fuels' benefits and problems | Zone: People & Places<br>Link: Population |

# Student Book Notes—*All in the Family*

## Synopsis

*All in the Family* explains how the world's creatures are classified. The book includes detailed coverage of the main phyla in the plant and animal kingdoms, and provides examples of how different living things interact.

## Vocabulary Development

*amoeba, antibiotic, biome, Carnivora, carnivore, chlorophyll, evolve, herbivore, mammal, mold, phloem, photosynthesis, spores, xylem*

### Challenges in the Text
scientific language

### Cross-Curricular Connections
life science; ecology

## Learning Outcomes

Students will:

1. be able to recall the names of the five kingdoms of living things.
2. explain the importance of the oxygen and carbon cycles.
3. know two reasons why most animals tend to live in groups.

## For Independent Readers

Provide these questions before students read the text:

- How many kinds of creatures are in the world?
- How are plants and animals different?
- What are the reasons some animal species have become extinct?
- Why are bacteria important?

## Visual Elements

Students have the opportunity to:

1. view sequential diagrams.
2. read charts with bullet points.
3. read and interpret nature cycle diagrams.
4. view double-page spreads.

## Purposes for Reading

Possible choices include:

1. to learn about how living things are classified.
2. to learn about the main phyla in the plant kingdom.
3. to learn about the main phyla in the animal kingdom.

## Critical Thinking

Students have the opportunity to:

1. form generalizations about the creatures in the animal kingdom.
2. summarize the changes that have taken place in the dog family.
3. classify, categorize, and organize information about living things.

## Special Features

- Check out "Profile" and learn how a hobby has led to the discovery of new species.
- "Try This!" explains how you can experiment with leftover food.
- Read "In Focus" and find out about life in an animal refuge.

## Guiding Learning

### Before Reading

Ask, *How do you describe the similarities and differences between cats and dogs?* Challenge students to compose a list of these similarities and differences.

### During Reading

Key text to guide:

**Pages 4–5:** Read these pages to students. Take time to discuss the classification system.

**Pages 6–7:** Share read these pages. Then help students understand the differences in the five kingdoms. Emphasize the importance of structure, mobility, and eating habits.

**Pages 8–11:** Say, *Read to the end of page 10 to find out what types of creatures make up the first three kingdoms.* (Share read with students needing support.) Discuss what students find out and then the importance of bacteria and fungi to people. Read through the procedural text on page 11. If possible, have students do the experiment.

**Pages 12–15:** Ensure students have a basic understanding of phyla and then have them read these pages. Discuss some differences among the animal and plant phyla.

**Pages 16–19:** Have students read pages 16 and 17 independently. Review their understanding of the classification system. Then ask, *How are different species of cats similar and different?* Have students read to the end of page 19 and follow with discussion about what they have learned.

**Pages 20–21:** Say, *Read to the end of page 21 and find out why there are so many different breeds of dogs.* Highlight natural evolution and crossbreeding.

**Pages 22–23:** Have students read these pages and discuss the two main reasons (companionship and protection) why most animals live in groups.

**Pages 24–25:** Highlight that the text is e-mails. Talk about some e-mail conventions (brevity, bullet points, attachments, etc.) and then have students read independently.

**Pages 26–27:** Share read these pages. Then ensure students understand the oxygen and carbon cycles.

**Pages 28–29:** Ask, *What is the main difference between human beings and other living things?* Have students read these pages and discuss.

### After Reading

Responding: Revisit the question posed in the Before Reading session. Help students work through the classification system to answer the question.

## Thinking Activity Master 1
### Creatures of the 5 Kingdoms: Classifying, Categorizing, and Organizing Information

Have students use the index, contents page, and glossary to find the correct kingdom for a range of creatures.

## www.rigbyinfoquest.com
### Zone: Plants & Animals
### Link: The Animal Kingdom

Students can research answers on the site:

1. What do you call a group of elephants?
2. How does an elephant use its trunk?
3. Which animals are related to beavers?
4. What is a beaver lodge?
5. Where do frogs fit in the animal kingdom?
6. How do frogs defend themselves?

### Learning Activities

Students can complete activities on the site:

- Organize the animals into their phylum.
- Make your own glossary by typing definitions for the words.

SITESEEING • PLANTS & ANIMALS •

**What do you call a group of elephants?**
Visit www.rigbyinfoquest.com
for more about THE ANIMAL KINGDOM.

# Creatures of the 5 Kingdoms

Name _____    Date _____

List the following creatures in the right kingdom.

anthropoda, bacteria, coral, bananas, mushrooms, amoeba, primates, molds, conifers, large single-celled creatures, yeast, small single-celled creatures, mosses, sea urchins

| The Monera Kingdom | The Protista Kingdom |
|---|---|
| | |

| The Fungi Kingdom | The Plant Kingdom |
|---|---|
| | |

**The Animal Kingdom**

# Nonfiction Assessment Record

**Book Title:** *All in the Family*

Student _____     Date _____

| | | |
|---|---|---|
| Say, *Read pages 4 and 5 silently.* Ask, *Why is it important to be able to classify living things?* | Was the student able to display an understanding of the importance? (Purpose for Reading 1) | ☐ |
| Say, *Read pages 12 and 13 silently.* Ask, *In what ways are ferns and mosses different?* | Did the student say one has a system of veins but the other doesn't? (Purpose for Reading 2) | ☐ |
| Say, *Read pages 14 and 15 silently.* Ask, *In what way are anthropoda and mollusca similar?* | Did the student understand that both are invertebrates? (Purpose for Reading 3) | ☐ |
| Ask, *How are animals different from other living things?* | Did the student mention many organized cells and mobility? (Critical Thinking 1) | ☐ |
| Say, *Read pages 20 and 21 silently.* Ask, *What are the main changes that have happened to dogs over the years?* | Was the student able to summarize the changes that have taken place? (Critical Thinking 2) | ☐ |
| Say, *Read pages 22 and 23 silently.* Ask, *What are two reasons most animals tend to live in groups?* | Did the student say for companionship and protection? (Learning Outcome 3) | ☐ |
| Say, *Read pages 26 and 27 silently.* Ask, *Why are the oxygen and carbon cycles very important?* | Did the student understand that all life is dependent on these cycles? (Learning Outcome 2) | ☐ |
| Ask, *Now that you have read the book, can you tell me the names of the five kingdoms of living things?* | Was the student able to recall all five kingdoms of living things? (Learning Outcome 1) | ☐ |

# Student Book Notes—*Built to Last*

**Synopsis**

*Built to Last* explores some styles of architecture seen throughout the ages. It highlights the reasons certain structures were built and how the use of technology has enabled architects to design new and innovative buildings.

**Vocabulary Development**

*architecture, Baroque, Mannerist, mausoleum, obelisk, philosophy, reinforced concrete, Renaissance, stonemason, symmetrical*

**Challenges in the Text**

architectural terms; historical perspective

**Cross-Curricular Connections**

social studies; fine arts

## Learning Outcomes

Students will:

1. be able to recall the main reason why the Tower of Pisa leans.
2. state why the Taj Mahal is considered one of the greatest works of architecture.
3. explain types of architecture used in St. Peter's Church in Rome.

## For Independent Readers

Provide these questions before students read the text:

- What do architects do?
- Which famous buildings do you know about, and what makes them special?
- When and where were the first skyscrapers built?
- How do people become architects?

## Visual Elements

Students have the opportunity to:

1. gain information from a variety of diagrams and photographs.
2. read and interpret a captioned map.
3. view double-page spreads.
4. read diagrams with labels.

## Purposes for Reading

Possible choices include:

1. to learn some of the reasons why people have built amazing buildings.
2. to learn about how technology has helped in the creation of new buildings.
3. to learn about the progression of building heights throughout the ages.

## Critical Thinking

Students have the opportunity to:

1. read and interpret a map with captions and illustrations.
2. form and justify opinions about innovative architectural styles.
3. locate and concisely summarize information in the form of "Do You Know?" answers.

## Special Features

- Read "Techtalk" to discover how the first concrete was made.
- Michelangelo was more than a famous artist. Read "Profile" to find out more.
- Where are the coldest hotels in the world? "In Focus" has the answer.

## Guiding Learning

### Before Reading

Discuss what students know about architecture and building. Ask, *How is architecture different in different types of buildings? What buildings have really impressed you? Why?*

### During Reading

Key text to guide:

**Pages 4–5:** Read these pages to students. Do they understand that this is a brochure? Discuss the content and the way the pages are laid out. Ask, *Why do you think people continued to build the tower?*

**Pages 6–7:** Share read the body text. Then have individual students locate different continents and read about the buildings on each of them. Point out that the buildings in the gray boxes will appear in the book.

**Pages 8–13:** Say, *Read to the end of page 13 and find three reasons people in the past built magnificent buildings.* (Share read sections of text with students needing support.) When students have finished, help them recall the concepts of order, harmony, and beauty. Ask, *What is special about the Taj Mahal?*

**Pages 14–19:** Because of the complexity of the text, share read or read these pages to students. Then review and have students point to examples in the illustrations of Renaissance, Mannerist, and Baroque styles of architecture. Discuss Michelangelo's contributions to several disciplines.

**Pages 20–23:** Have students read these pages independently. Discuss the advances in technology that have allowed innovation to take place. Challenge students to form and justify opinions about the architecture on these pages.

**Pages 24–27:** Say, *Read to the end of page 27 and find out how technology has enabled the building of stronger and taller structures.* When students have finished, discuss the use of elevators, prefabrication, and cranes in the construction of tall buildings.

**Pages 28–29:** Either share read or read these pages to students. Ask, *Why do you think people go to the trouble of constructing temporary hotels made of ice?*

### After Reading

Responding: Invite students to use the index and find the building that most impresses them. Then challenge them to state why they think their chosen buildings are the most impressive.

## Thinking Activity Master 2
### Do You Know? Locating and Concisely Summarizing Information

Talk about the way in which authors sometimes write information in the form of "Do You Know?" answers. Discuss how these are written by using concise language and including the most important or interesting facts about a specific topic.

## www.rigbyinfoquest.com
### Zone: People & Places
### Link: Buildings

Students can research answers on the site:

1. How do building designs keep sports fans happy?
2. Why is the Tower of London famous?
3. How was the design of Casa Milá inspired by nature?

### Learning Activities

Students can complete activities on the site:

- Play the steps and ladders game.
- Design a safety poster for a construction site.

How do building designs keep sports fans happy? Visit www.rigbyinfoquest.com for more about BUILDINGS.

# Do You Know?

Name _____     Date _____

Use the index in *Built to Last* to find information. Then reread and write an exciting "Do You Know?" fact for each of the buildings below.

### Taj Mahal
_____

_____

_____

_____

### Hall of Supreme Harmony
_____

_____

_____

_____

### Built to Last

### St. Peter's Church in Rome
_____

_____

_____

_____

### Sydney Opera House
_____

_____

_____

_____

### Colosseum
_____

_____

_____

_____

# Nonfiction Assessment Record

**Book Title:** *Built to Last*

Student _____   Date _____

| | | |
|---|---|---|
| Say, *Read pages 4 and 5 silently.*<br>Ask, *What is the main reason the Tower of Pisa leans?* | Did the student understand the cause was erosion or sinking soil? (Learning Outcome 1) | ☐ |
| Say, *Read pages 6 and 7 silently.*<br>Ask, *Why are some of the captions in purple boxes, while the others aren't?* | Did the student state that the purple caption information appears only on these pages? (Critical Thinking 1) | ☐ |
| Ask, *What are two reasons why people build amazing buildings?* | Was the student able to supply at least two different reasons? (Purpose for Reading 1) | ☐ |
| Say, *Read pages 12 and 13 silently.*<br>Ask, *Why is the Taj Mahal considered one of the greatest buildings?* | Did the student mention the concept of symmetry? (Learning Outcome 2) | ☐ |
| Say, *Read pages 15 and 16 silently.*<br>Ask, *Where in St. Peter's Church are the Mannerist and Baroque styles used?* | Could the student locate the appropriate sections? (Learning Outcome 3) | ☐ |
| Say, *Read pages 20 and 21 silently.*<br>Ask, *Why do you like or dislike the style of these museums?* | Could the student form and justify an appropriate opinion? (Critical Thinking 2) | ☐ |
| Say, *Read pages 24 through 27 silently.*<br>Ask, *Where can the tallest tower in the world be found?* | Did the student say Toronto or Canada? (Purpose for Reading 3) | ☐ |
| Ask, *What are two ways technology has helped in the creation of taller buildings?* | Was the student able to recall at least two ways? (Purpose for Reading 2) | ☐ |

# Student Book Notes—*Close Up on Careers*

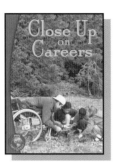

**Synopsis**

*Close Up on Careers* explores a variety of different jobs and profiles some of the people involved in them. The book includes some suggestions for beginning to think about future careers, and it highlights the huge range of choices available.

**Vocabulary Development**
*contractor, curator, font, live broadcast, professional, voluntary work*

**Challenges in the Text**
technical language; biographical text

**Cross-Curricular Connections**
social studies; science

## Learning Outcomes

Students will:

1. explain how to begin thinking about a future career.
2. recall ways computers are used in everyday life.
3. display an understanding of the main categories of scientists.

## For Independent Readers

Provide these questions before students read the text:

- When should you start planning a career?
- Which present-day careers didn't exist fifty years ago?
- Why do people now often change careers?
- How can you find out more about careers?

## Visual Elements

Students have the opportunity to:

1. read illustrations with labels.
2. view cartoon-style illustrations.
3. view a variety of photographs and illustrations.
4. view double-page spreads.

## Purposes for Reading

Possible choices include:

1. to learn about some types of media.
2. to learn about careers involved in the care of people.
3. to learn about the careers of some famous people.

## Critical Thinking

Students have the opportunity to:

1. match job descriptions with a range of different jobs.
2. compare the roles of veterinarians and doctors.
3. organize and summarize information about a possible future career.

## Special Features

- Start thinking about your future. "In Focus" will get you started.
- Make your own magazine. "Try This!" shows you how.
- Check out "Profile" and discover how a childhood hobby became a career.
- How many careers can you find? Test your skills with "Fact Finder."

## Guiding Learning
### Before Reading
Read the title to students. Ask, *How do people choose their careers? Do people always end up in the job they expected?* Make a list of common responses to these questions for the "After Reading" session.

### During Reading
Key text to guide:

**Pages 4–5:** Ask, *What are some ways people can start thinking about a future career?* Have students respond and then read these pages independently.

**Pages 6–13:** Say, *Read to the end of page 13 and find out about some different media careers.* (Share read with students needing support.) When students have finished, discuss the different kinds of jobs that are involved in the communication industry. Then turn to page 9 and choose students to match the jobs with their descriptions.

**Pages 14–17:** Ask, *How many different kinds of health professionals do you know?* Give students time to respond before having them read to the end of page 17. When students have finished, reread page 14 and discuss some of the more obscure careers.

**Pages 18–21:** Say, *Although doctors' and veterinarians' patients are different, their professional roles have many similarities. Read to the end of page 21 and find out what some of these are.* When students have finished, discuss some of the similarities and differences.

**Pages 22–25:** Share read these pages with students. Discuss the three main areas of science, and then help students understand what each of the scientists on page 23 does. Highlight the fact that each of the scientists on pages 24 and 25 became interested in their respective fields at a relatively young age.

**Pages 26–27:** Say, *Some careers may seem stranger than others. Read pages 26 and 27 and discover a few.* When students have finished, have them select their least likely career from these pages.

**Pages 28–29:** Challenge students to find and list as many different careers as they can.

### After Reading
Responding: Reread the responses from the "Before Reading" session. Then invite students to consider and amend their answers based on what they have read.

## Thinking Activity Master 3
### My Dream Career: Organizing and Summarizing Information
Read through the activity with students. Ensure students understand that although they may change their minds when they get older, many people end up in careers that they started thinking about when they were quite young.

## www.rigbyinfoquest.com
### Zone: People & Places
### Link: Careers
Students can research answers on the site:
1. What is a foley artist?
2. What are careers in dance and related arts?
3. What are some sports careers?
4. What is an oceanographer?
5. How do oceanographers conduct research?

### Learning Activities
Students can complete activities on the site:
- Write a newspaper advertisement for help wanted.
- Fill in the speech balloons for the comic strip.

# My Dream Career

Name _____    Date _____

Using what you have read and observed, write to record about a career.

My dream career: _____

Qualities I already have for the work: _____

_____

_____

Other qualities I would need: _____

_____

_____

Education required (what kind, where, how long, etc.): _____

_____

_____

Why I would choose this career: _____

_____

_____

_____

"Plan B"—Three other possible careers, just in case the first one doesn't work out, and why they interest me:

_____        _____

_____        _____

_____        _____

# Nonfiction Assessment Record

**Book Title:** *Close Up on Careers*

Student _____     Date _____

| | |
|---|---|
| Say, *Read pages 4 and 5 silently.*<br>Ask, *Why should you be the person who makes the final decision on your future career?* | Did the student understand that she or he knows her or himself better than anyone else? (Learning Outcome 1) ☐ |
| Say, *Read pages 6 through 11 silently.*<br>Ask, *How are electronic media and print media different?* | Was the student able to specify the main difference between the two? (Purpose for Reading 1) ☐ |
| Ask, *What are the different jobs of television producers and directors?* | Was the student able to match the information? (Critical Thinking 1) ☐ |
| Say, *Read page 12 silently.*<br>Ask, *What are three ways we commonly use our computers?* | Was the student able to recall at least three different ways? (Learning Outcome 2) ☐ |
| Say, *Read pages 14 through 19 silently.*<br>Ask, *What are four professions involved with helping people?* | Was the student able to locate the appropriate information on page 16? (Purpose for Reading 2) ☐ |
| Ask, *How are the roles of doctors and veterinarians similar and different?* | Did the student specify at least one similarity and one difference? (Critical Thinking 2) ☐ |
| Say, *Read pages 22 through 25 silently.*<br>Ask, *What is the main difference between life science and physical science?* | Did the student display an understanding of the main difference? (Learning Outcome 3) ☐ |
| Ask, *How are the careers of Scott Hocknull and Margaret Mead similar?* | Did the student recognize the early start, the passion involved, or a similar concept? (Purpose for Reading 3) ☐ |

# Student Book Notes—*Cogs in the Wheel*

### Synopsis

*Cogs in the Wheel* outlines the major developments of the Industrial Revolution. This book features the most significant people and inventions of the period, and it highlights the conditions faced by workers and their families in the new industrialized cities.

### Vocabulary Development

*assembly line, crop rotation, developing country, enclosure, industrialization, interchangeable part, lock, mass production, mechanization, patent, pauper apprentice, selective breeding, synthetic, textile*

### Challenges in the Text

historical perspective; biographies

### Cross-Curricular Connections

social studies; physical science; technology

## Learning Outcomes

Students will:

1. be able to explain what the Industrial Revolution was.
2. recall the conditions faced by people in the new industrialized cities.
3. display an understanding of the ongoing nature of the Industrial Revolution.

## For Independent Readers

Provide these questions before students read the text:

- What is a revolution?
- How did the machines of the Industrial Revolution change people's lives?
- Why did people start moving from rural to urban settings?
- What are the benefits of mass production?

## Visual Elements

Students have the opportunity to:

1. interpret illustrations with labels.
2. read a pictorial graph.
3. gain information from a variety of photographs and illustrations.

## Purposes for Reading

Possible choices include:

1. to learn about the conditions that led to the Industrial Revolution.
2. to learn about the most important advances of the Industrial Revolution.
3. to learn about the main features of the Second Industrial Revolution.

## Critical Thinking

Students have the opportunity to:

1. form generalizations about the Industrial Revolution in America.
2. form and justify opinions about the need for child labor.
3. use text organizers to locate, sequence, and record information in a time line.

## Special Features

- "In Focus" explains why the Industrial Revolution started in Britain.
- Who invented the steam engine? "Profile" has the information.
- Why was the telegraph very important? Read "Time Link" and find out.
- "Fast Facts" explains just how fast the speediest trains were in the 1800s.

## Guiding Learning

### Before Reading

Have students view the cover photograph. Invite them to share any information they know about early machines.

### During Reading

Key text to guide:

**Pages 4–5:** Read these pages to students. Help them understand the significance of the changes brought about by the Industrial Revolution.

**Pages 6–7:** Say, *Read to the end of page 7 and find out how the Industrial Revolution started.* When students have finished, discuss some of the improvements in agriculture.

**Pages 8–11:** Say, *The invention of the spinning jenny and the steam engine greatly changed the daily lives of people. Read to the end of page 11 to find out how.* When students have finished, discuss these inventions and the importance of water and coal power.

**Pages 12–15:** Have students read these pages independently. (Share read with students needing support.) Help students recall and discuss the unique conditions that led to rapid industrialization in America.

**Pages 16–17:** Say, *Read to the end of page 17. Find out what special problem Canada had and how it was solved.* Discuss the functions of locks and the development of the Welland Canal.

**Pages 18–19:** Have students read these pages independently and then comment on the growing need for speed.

**Pages 20–23:** Say, *Read to the end of page 23 and find out what life and work was like for families that moved to rapidly growing cities.* Discuss the difficult conditions and the use of child labor. Help students understand the graph on page 20.

**Pages 24–27:** Have students read these pages independently. Then talk about the importance of the telephone, the electric light bulb, and the assembly line in the huge production increases.

**Pages 28–29:** Say, *The Industrial Revolution didn't happen everywhere at the same time. Read to the end of page 29 to find out where it continues to happen and some of the problems associated with it.* Then discuss what students have found out.

### After Reading

Responding: Invite students to suggest and justify what they consider to be the most important invention of the Industrial Revolution.

## Thinking Activity Master 4
### Industrial Revolution Time Line: Locating, Sequencing, and Recording Information

Read through the instructions on the Thinking Activity worksheet with the students. Then have them use the text organizers in the book to help them complete the time line.

## www.rigbyinfoquest.com
### Zone: Past & Future
### Link: The Industrial Revolution

Students can research answers on the site:
1. Who wrote about child labor?
2. Why was author Frances Trollope criticized?
3. Who worked in coal mines?
4. How did animals work in coal mines?

### Learning Activities

Students can complete activities on the site:

- Answer the questions to build a train track.
- Write diary entries for a child working in the coal mines.

**SITESEEING · PAST & FUTURE ·**

**Who wrote about child labor?**
Visit www.rigbyinfoquest.com for more about THE INDUSTRIAL REVOLUTION.

# Industrial Revolution Time Line

Name _____    Date _____

Use the index and contents page of *Cogs in the Wheel* to find the dates of the events below. Write each event in the appropriate dated box.

First moving assembly line       Pacific Railroad completed      Jane Addams dies

Chicago population is 1,000,000   Welland Canal opens            First telephone call

James Watt born                  Morse Code invented            First American oil well

St. Lawrence Seaway opens

| 1736 | 1876 |
|------|------|
| 1829 | 1890 |
| 1830s | 1914 |
| 1859 | 1935 |
| 1869 | 1959 |

# Nonfiction Assessment Record

**Book Title:** *Cogs in the Wheel*

Student _____     Date _____

| | | |
|---|---|---|
| Say, *Read pages 4 through 7 silently.* Ask, *How was the Industrial Revolution different from other types of revolutions?* | Did the student indicate that this was a revolution in technology? (Learning Outcome 1) | ☐ |
| Ask, *What was life like for most people before the Industrial Revolution?* | Was the student able to provide a brief summary of conditions? (Purpose for Reading 1) | ☐ |
| Say, *Read pages 12 and 13 silently.* Ask, *Why did the Industrial Revolution spread so quickly in America?* | Was the student able to form an appropriate generalization? (Critical Thinking 1) | ☐ |
| Say, *Read pages 20 through 23 silently.* Ask, *What were conditions like for people in industrialized cities?* | Was the student able to recall the main conditions in these cities? (Learning Outcome 2) | ☐ |
| Ask, *Should children have been allowed to work in factories? Why/Why not?* | Was the student able to form and justify an opinion? (Critical Thinking 2) | ☐ |
| Say, *Read pages 24 and 25 silently.* Ask, *How was the Second Industrial Revolution different from the first?* | Was the student able to specify the differences? (Purpose for Reading 3) | ☐ |
| Say, *Read pages 28 and 29 silently.* Ask, *What are some of the problems faced by developing countries?* | Was the student able to recall at least two different problems? (Learning Outcome 3) | ☐ |
| Ask, *What do you think was the most important development of the Industrial Revolution? Why?* | Was the student able to specify about an appropriate development? (Purpose for Reading 2) | ☐ |

# Student Book Notes—*Digging for History*

## Synopsis

*Digging for History* features the world of archaeology. The text explores how dig sites are located and worked, both on land and under the seas. The book also highlights the rise and fall of the Mayan civilization. A brief look at the future of archaeology is taken.

**Vocabulary Development**
*analysis, anthropologist, conquistador, epigraph, Mesoamérica, nonperishable, paleontologist, plaza, preserve, radioactive, sedimentary, survey*

**Challenges in the Text**
time line; historical perspective

**Cross-Curricular Connections**
social studies; technology

## Learning Outcomes

Students will:

1. be able to state why it is important to understand the past.
2. display an understanding of why temples were important to the Mayans.
3. be able to recall ways that archaeologists discover new sites.

## For Independent Readers

Provide these questions before students read the text:

- What are the main tasks carried out by archaeologists?
- What do paleontologists do?
- Do you think there are more ancient civilizations to be discovered?
- Why are artifacts important?

## Visual Elements

Students have the opportunity to:

1. view sequential diagrams.
2. read a range of maps.
3. interpret a variety of photographs and illustrations.
4. view double-page spreads.

## Purposes for Reading

Possible choices include:

1. to learn how paleontologists discover and date dinosaur fossils.
2. to learn the steps undertaken by archaeologists at a dig site.
3. to learn about the rise and fall of the Mayan civilization.

## Critical Thinking

Students have the opportunity to:

1. compare and contrast the roles of land and underwater archaeologists.
2. form and justify opinions about the fate of artifacts from the *Titanic*.
3. compose and record information about what they would include in a personal time capsule.

## Special Features

- Check out "Profile" to find out who discovered the oldest footprints.
- Why did the *Titanic* sink? "In Focus" has all the answers.
- Why do people bury time capsules? Read "Try This!" and think about what you would include in a capsule.

## Guiding Learning

### Before Reading

Help students recall their studies about any ancient civilizations. Ask, *How do we find out about these civilizations? How do people know where to look for them?*

### During Reading

Key text to guide:

**Pages 4–5:** Read these pages to students. Discuss the importance of understanding the past in order to plan for the future.

**Pages 6–9:** Ask, *How do archaeologists know where to look for artifacts? What do they do when they find the site?* Have students independently read these pages. When students have finished, review the six steps on pages 8 and 9. Talk about the great care taken to preserve a site.

**Pages 10–11:** Share read the body text on these pages. Ensure that students understand the significance of Leakey's discovery. Then ask, *What qualities do you think a good archaeologist has?* Have students read the appropriate text on page 11 and comment.

**Pages 12–13:** Have students read the body text on these pages independently. When finished, discuss the role of paleontologists. Then read the "Dinosaur Dating" text to students and discuss the two types of dating.

**Pages 14–19:** Read page 14 to students, and then ask *How do archeologists work under the ocean to discover similar wrecks and artifacts?* Have students read independently to the end of page 18. Then discuss the similarities and differences in land and underwater archaeology. Read page 19 to students. Ask, *Do you think these artifacts should be displayed for the public? Why/Why not?*

**Pages 20–25:** Say, *Read to the end of page 25 and find out who the ancient Mayans were, how they lived, and what became of them.* (Share read with students needing support.) When students have finished, discuss the importance of temples and the problem with the conquistadors. Reread the time line with students.

**Pages 26–29:** Read pages 26 and 27 to students and then have them read to the end of page 29. Discuss the importance of preserving artifacts for future generations.

### After Reading

Responding: Have students discuss what they have learned about the work of archaeologists. Ask, *Do you think there are still ancient civilizations to discover?*

## Thinking Activity Master 5

### My Personal Time Capsule: Composing and Recording Personal Information

Reread page 29 with students. Have them discuss what they would include in a personal time capsule before they complete the activity.

## www.rigbyinfoquest.com

**Zone: Science & Technology**

**Link: Archaeology**

Students can research answers on the site:

1. How do archaeologists dig up the truth?
2. How can archaeology help solve a mystery?
3. What happened to the Anasazi?
4. Where can dinosaur fossils be found?
5. How did dinosaur fossils form?

### Learning Activities

Students can complete activities on the site:

- Piece together the bones and discover a dinosaur.
- See how many words you can discover in the wordfind.

How do archaeologists dig up the truth?
Visit **www.rigbyinfoquest.com** for more about ARCHAEOLOGY.

# My Personal Time Capsule

Name _____    Date _____

Think about what you would put in a personal time capsule. Then use the headings below to help you organize these items.

| Photographs | Personal Information |
|:---:|:---:|
| | |

| Family Information | Favorite Things<br>(food, entertainment, music, sports, etc.) |
|:---:|:---:|
| | |

| Hopes for My Own Future | How I Think Life Will Be<br>in 100 Years |
|:---:|:---:|
| | |

# Nonfiction Assessment Record

**Book Title:** *Digging for History*

Student _____    Date _____

| | | |
|---|---|---|
| Say, *Read pages 4 and 5 silently.* Ask, *Why is it important for us to understand the past?* | Did the student understand how an awareness of the past helps us to plan the future? (Learning Outcome 1) | ☐ |
| Say, *Read pages 6 and 7 silently.* Ask, *What are two different ways archaeologists discover new sites?* | Was the student able to specify at least two different ways? (Learning Outcome 3) | ☐ |
| Say, *Read pages 8 and 9 silently.* Ask, *How do archaeologists remove artifacts from dig sites?* | Was the student able to specify the information from step 4 on page 9? (Purpose for Reading 2) | ☐ |
| Say, *Read pages 12 and 13 silently.* Ask, *What are the two main ways paleontologists date dinosaur fossils?* | Did the student imply "rate of decay" and "depth of fossil" or similar ideas? (Purpose for Reading 1) | ☐ |
| Say, *Read pages 15 through 19 silently.* Ask, *What are two ways archaeology on land and under the ocean are different?* | Was the student able to offer two appropriate differences? (Critical Thinking 1) | ☐ |
| Ask, *Why or why not do you think the* Titanic *artifacts should be publicly displayed?* | Was the student able to form and justify a reasonable opinion? (Critical Thinking 2) | ☐ |
| Say, *Read pages 20 through 25 silently.* Ask, *Why were the temples very important to the Mayans?* | Did the student display an understanding of the importance of these temples? (Learning Outcome 2) | ☐ |
| Ask, *What was the main reason for the fall of the Mayan civilization?* | Did the student understand that disease, not conflict, was the major cause? (Purpose for Reading 3) | ☐ |

# Student Book Notes—*Escape!*

**Synopsis**

From the dangerous journeys through the Underground Railroad to the courageous decision made by a trapped climber, *Escape!* highlights incredible escapes throughout history. Readers can learn much about the people and animals involved in those escapes.

**Vocabulary Development**
*Allies, French Resistance, Gestapo, political oppression, Special Operations Executive, Underground Railroad*
**Challenges in the Text**
biographical text
**Cross-Curricular Connections**
social studies—history

## Learning Outcomes

Students will:

1. recall at least two dangers associated with the *Apollo 13* mission.
2. explain the difficulties faced by runaway slaves in the 1800s.
3. display an understanding of why dogs are useful in many rescue situations.

## For Independent Readers

Provide these questions before students read the text:

- Who is your personal hero? Why?
- What are some qualities most heroes have in common?
- Have you or anyone you know ever needed to escape from danger?
- Why do some people choose to face danger?

## Visual Elements

Students have the opportunity to:

1. gain information from a variety of diagrams and photographs.
2. read cartoon-style text.
3. view captioned diagrams.
4. read an information checklist.

## Purposes for Reading

Possible choices include:

1. to learn about several people who have escaped danger.
2. to learn about people who risked their lives to help others.
3. to learn about the purpose and format of a bibliography.

## Critical Thinking

Students have the opportunity to:

1. form generalizations about the qualities required to survive a disaster.
2. form and justify opinions about escapes from POW camps.
3. recognize important information while composing interview questions and possible responses.

## Special Features

- "In the News" tells the lengths one man went to save his own life.
- The need to pay attention to your parents is well illustrated in "Time Link."
- Check out "In Focus" and read about one of the all-time-greatest escapes.
- Read "Profile" and discover a woman who risked her life to save many others.

## Guiding Learning

### Before Reading

Ask, *Why do some people risk their lives to save others?* Have students discuss their responses. Talk about some of the qualities these people have in common.

### During Reading

Key text to guide:

**Pages 4–5:** Read these pages to students. Help them understand that the will to live is incredibly strong, as is the will to help others.

**Pages 6–7:** Say, *Read pages 6 and 7 to find out how 62 people survived what appeared to be an impossible situation.* When students have finished, talk about the reaction of the crowd of onlookers.

**Pages 8–13:** Have students read these pages independently. (Share read with those needing further support.) Then discuss the problems encountered and the team approach to solving those problems.

**Pages 14–15:** Have students read the body text on page 14, and then read the "Time Link" section to students. Challenge them to compose a moral for the myth.

**Pages 16–17:** Highlight the format of these pages, and then have students read them. Ask, *What was amazing about this escape?* Discuss the students' responses to the question.

**Pages 18–21:** Say, *Read to the end of page 21.* Find out about the risks involved for slaves and for those who helped them escape. When finished, talk about the will to be free and the bravery of those who helped.

**Pages 22–25:** Say, *Read to the end of page 25 and find out how one very brave woman risked her life to help others.* Then help students understand that Nancy Wake could have chosen to sit out the war in relative luxury but decided instead to help others.

**Pages 26–29:** Ask, *Why are dogs very well suited to search and rescue work?* Have students independently read these pages. Discuss the superior tracking skills of certain types of dogs.

**Page 31:** Discuss the nature and format of bibliographies. Remind students that a bibliography lists the publications which the author used and provides a list of references the reader can use to find out more about a topic.

### After Reading

Responding: Now that students have read the book, have them revisit the question posed in the "Before Reading" section.

## Thinking Activity Master 6

### Nancy Wake Interview: Recognizing Important Information

Demonstrate an interview (question and answer) format. Reread pages 22 through 25 with students. Then have them write interview questions for Nancy Wake and create possible answers.

## www.rigbyinfoquest.com

**Zone: People & Places**

**Link: Escapes**

Students can research answers on the site:

1. How were people hidden inside "safe houses"?
2. How did escaping slaves find the route to freedom?
3. How did people escape from Colditz Castle?
4. What was the Colditz Glider?
5. How have mannequins been used in escapes?

### Learning Activities

Students can complete activities on the site:

- Write a story about an escape from Colditz Castle.
- Fill in the speech balloons to complete a comic strip.

SITESEEING • PEOPLE & PLACES

How were people hidden inside "safe houses"?
Visit www.rigbyinfoquest.com
for more about ESCAPES.

# Nancy Wake Interview

Name _____     Date _____

Think of four questions that you would ask Nancy Wake if you could interview her. Then write what you think she might answer.

Question 1: _____

Response: _____

_____

_____

Question 2: _____

Response: _____

_____

_____

Question 3: _____

Response: _____

_____

_____

Question 4: _____

Response: _____

_____

_____

What are three qualities that you think Nancy Wake displayed? When?

1. _____

2. _____

3. _____

© 2004 Rigby—Rigby InfoQuest

# Nonfiction Assessment Record

**Book Title:** *Escape!*

Student _____     Date _____

| | |
|---|---|
| Say, *Read pages 8 through 13 silently.* Ask, *What were two dangers faced by the Apollo 13 astronauts?* | Was the student able to recall at least two different dangers? (Learning Outcome 1) ☐ |
| Ask, *What qualities did the astronauts have that helped them survive?* | Was the student able to specify qualities like remaining calm, problem solving, bravery, etc.? (Critical Thinking 1) ☐ |
| Say, *Read pages 16 and 17 silently.* Ask, *Why or why don't you think these POWs should have risked their lives?* | Was the student able to form and justify an opinion? (Critical Thinking 2) ☐ |
| Say, *Read pages 18 through 21 silently.* Ask, *What were some of the difficulties faced by these slaves?* | Was the student able to specify at least two different difficulties? (Learning Outcome 2) ☐ |
| Ask, *What service did people such as Levi and Catherine Coffin provide?* | Did the student understand the importance of the safe houses? (Purpose for Reading 2) ☐ |
| Say, *Read pages 26 and 27 silently.* Ask, *Why are some dogs very useful in many search and rescue situations?* | Did the student understand the importance of the heightened senses of dogs? (Learning Outcome 3) ☐ |
| Say, *Look at the bibliography on page 31.* Ask, *What is one reason authors sometimes include a bibliography?* | Was the student able to provide at least one reason? (Purpose for Reading 3) ☐ |
| Say, *Choose one person or group of people from the book. Tell me what was special about what they did.* | Was the student able to summarize the importance of what was done? (Purpose for Reading 1) ☐ |

# Student Book Notes—*Famous Faces*

### Synopsis

*Famous Faces* features some of the most memorable people from different walks of life. The book explores fleeting fame and fame that stands the test of time. It also highlights the role of the media in portraying the ways people are perceived.

### Vocabulary Development

*alias, annex, caricature, celebrity, commemorate, head of state, heritage, Holocaust, icon, immortal, infamous, media, memento, monarch, prodigy*

### Challenges in the Text

biographical text

### Cross-Curricular Connections

social studies—history

## Learning Outcomes

Students will:

1. explain why certain famous faces stand the test of time.
2. display an understanding of the effects of the media on famous people.
3. understand the ongoing contributions made by gifted and talented people.

## For Independent Readers

Provide these questions before students read the text:

- Why are some faces instantaneously recognizable?
- How does the media affect fame?
- Do you have a famous family member?
- Why doesn't fame last for some people?

## Visual Elements

Students have the opportunity to:

1. view cartoon-style illustrations.
2. read text in a puzzle format.
3. view a variety of photographs and illustrations.

## Purposes for Reading

Possible choices include:

1. to learn some ways historical figures are remembered.
2. to learn about some ways bravery is commemorated.
3. to learn about different ways beauty is perceived.

## Critical Thinking

Students have the opportunity to:

1. form a generalization about the importance of Anne Frank's diary.
2. form and justify opinions about famous people's right to privacy.
3. compose and summarize information in the form of a report.

## Special Features

- "Time Link" shows you where you can step on your favorite stars.
- Read "In Focus" and find out how a simple diary became very important.
- Check out "Try This!" and learn how to draw faces.
- Should famous people have their privacy? Have your say with "What's Your Opinion?"

## Guiding Learning

### Before Reading

Have students read through the index entries. Ask, *Which of these people have you heard of? Why are they famous? Do they have anything in common?* Give time for students to respond and discuss.

### During Reading

Key text to guide:

**Pages 4–5:** Read page 4 to students. Discuss the qualities that many famous people have and the role of the media in the portrayal of currently famous people.

**Pages 6–9:** Ask, *What are some of the ways historical figures are remembered?* Then have students read to the end of page 9 and discuss the different ways people are remembered.

**Pages 10–11:** Have students read these pages independently. Ask, *Why do you think the New Zealand government decided to break tradition by putting Hillary's face on the five-dollar bill?*

**Pages 12–15:** Have students read pages 12 and 13 independently and then share read pages 14 and 15. Challenge students to discuss how each of these people were heroes for very different reasons. Ask, *Why do you think Anne Frank's diary remains important today?*

**Pages 16–19:** Say, *Some people achieve fame for what they do and others simply for how they look. Read to the end of page 19 to find out how these very different people became famous.* When students have finished, challenge them to discuss different concepts of beauty.

**Pages 20–21:** Have students read these pages independently. If appropriate, give them time to try drawing their own cartoon faces.

**Pages 22–25:** Ask, *In what ways does the media affect how we perceive famous people?* Then have students read these pages independently. Discuss the pros and cons of the media's treatment of celebrities.

**Pages 26–27:** Ask, *Can everyone be famous, if only for a short time?* Have students discuss this and then read these pages independently.

**Pages 28–29:** Give students time to match the sayings with the portraits.

### After Reading

Responding: Have students choose the person from the book whom they consider made the most significant contribution. Have them justify their responses.

## Thinking Activity Master 7
### My Moment of Fame: Composing and Summarizing Information

Discuss how anyone can be famous for a short time, even if it involves something simple like writing a popular story or rescuing a lost pet. Read through the thinking activity before students complete the task.

## www.rigbyinfoquest.com
### Zone: People & Places
### Link: Famous People

Students can research answers on the site:

1. Who makes wax models of famous people?
2. Who was Louis Pasteur?
3. Why was Picasso famous?
4. How can we learn about famous people?

### Learning Activities

Students can complete activities on the site:

- Match each famous person and caption.
- Choose a famous person and write a profile.

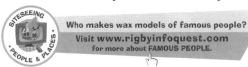

# My Moment of Fame

Name _____     Date _____

Think of a time that you felt proud of something you did. This was one of your moments of fame.

My moment of fame: _____

Date and time: _____

Names of witnesses (if any): _____

_____

What actually happened: _____

_____

_____

_____

_____

_____

_____

My feelings: _____

_____

_____

The qualities that I think this moment of fame shows I have:_____

_____

_____

_____

_____

# Nonfiction Assessment Record

**Book Title:** *Famous Faces*

Student _____  Date _____

| | | |
|---|---|---|
| Say, *Read pages 4 and 5 silently.*<br>Ask, *Why do some people continue to be famous over many years?* | Was the student able to form an appropriate generalization? (Learning Outcome 1) | ☐ |
| Say, *Read pages 6 through 9 silently.*<br>Ask, *What are some of the ways historical figures are remembered?* | Was the student able to recall at least three different ways? (Purpose for Reading 1) | ☐ |
| Say, *Read pages 12 through 15 silently.*<br>Ask, *How is Nelson's bravery still remembered today?* | Did the student supply two or three different ways? (Purpose for Reading 2) | ☐ |
| Ask, *Why do you think that Anne Frank's diary continues to be widely read?* | Did the student understand the power of a personal account, especially from a child? (Critical Thinking 1) | ☐ |
| Say, *Read pages 16 and 17 silently.*<br>Ask, *What did Albert Einstein and Marie Curie have in common?* | Did the student understand that each of their contributions are ongoing? (Learning Outcome 3) | ☐ |
| Say, *Read pages 18 and 19 silently.*<br>Ask, *Why do different people have different views of beauty?* | Was the student able to form an appropriate generalization? (Purpose for Reading 3) | ☐ |
| Say, *Read pages 24 and 25 silently.*<br>Ask, *How does the media effect the way we regard famous people?* | Did the student understand the power of the media in promoting or damaging reputations? (Learning Outcome 2) | ☐ |
| Ask, *Do you think famous people have a right to privacy? Why/Why not?* | Was the student able to form and justify an opinion? (Critical Thinking 2) | ☐ |

# Student Book Notes—*Giants of the Deep*

## Synopsis

*Giants of the Deep* explores the great fish and mammals of the ocean depths. The book highlights the successes of some predators and the decline of several species. It includes a gatefold section showing creatures that live at different ocean levels.

**Vocabulary Development**
*barb, bioluminescence, camouflage, cartilage, dredge, echolocation, fathom, hull, moratorium, overfish, pack ice, prehistoric, sustainable*

**Challenges in the Text**
ocean layer diagram

**Cross-Curricular Connections**
life science; ecology

## Learning Outcomes

Students will:

1. be able to state at least two natural dangers facing ocean ships.
2. display an understanding of why sharks have been very successful.
3. recall how some countries are working to preserve ocean habitats.

## For Independent Readers

Provide these questions before students read the text:

• Do sea monsters really exist?
• Why are the world's largest animals found in oceans?
• Why are there parts of the ocean we know very little about?
• Will humans ever live underwater?

## Visual Elements

Students have the opportunity to:

1. gain information from a variety of diagrams and photographs.
2. read diagrams with labels.
3. read a sequential diagram with captions.
4. view a map with a key.

## Purposes for Reading

Possible choices include:

1. to learn about some kinds of whales.
2. to learn about the way sharks are classified.
3. to learn about the creatures in different layers of the oceans.

## Critical Thinking

Students have the opportunity to:

1. summarize some of the differences between cetaceans and fish.
2. form and justify opinions about whaling and the decline of whales.
3. locate and match important information about sea creatures.

## Special Features

• "In the News" explores the fascinating world of the giant squid.
• Read about a giant iceberg. "Earth Watch" has the amazing facts.
• Try your luck at blending in. "Try This!" tells you how.
• Should people hunt whales? Have your say with "What's Your Opinion?"

# Guiding Learning

## Before Reading

Discuss what students know about giant sea creatures. Ask, *Which creatures do people most fear? Why? Which creatures are endangered? What can we do to help them?* Record student responses for later.

## During Reading

Key text to guide:

**Pages 4–5:** Read these pages aloud. Discuss the stories told about sea monsters and what we now know about ocean depths.

**Pages 6–7:** Say, *What other dangers do sailors face?* Have students read these pages independently and then talk about the dangers of huge waves and icebergs.

**Pages 8–11:** Say, *Read to the end of page 11. Find out what cetaceans are and the differences between toothed and baleen whales.* When students have finished, discuss the differences between cetaceans and fish. Highlight the eating habits of the two main types of whales.

**Pages 12–13:** Have students read these pages independently. Talk about what most rays have in common.

**Pages 14–19:** Read pages 14 and 19 to students. Help students understand the difficulty facing the crew of *Challenger* because of the limited access to technology. Then turn to the gatefold. Share read these pages. Help students locate specific animals, and discuss how each are suited to a specific layer of an ocean. Ask, *Why can very few creatures exist in ocean trenches?*

**Pages 20–25:** Invite students to discuss their understandings and assumptions about sharks. Then have students read to the end of page 25. (Share read with students needing support.) When students have finished, help them understand the classification of sharks and some of the myths surrounding them.

**Pages 26–27:** Have students read these pages independently. Invite them to consider the "What's Your Opinion?" information to state and justify opinions.

**Pages 28–29:** Ask, *What is the main reason the world's oceans need to be protected?* After students have responded, have them read these pages and discuss.

## After Reading

Responding: Revisit the questions from the "Before Reading" session. Encourage students to respond again to these questions and locate text to justify their views by using the contents page and index.

# Thinking Activity Master 8
## Ocean Life: Locating and Matching Information

Review how the contents page, glossary, and index can be used to locate specific information. Hand out the worksheets, highlight the example, and discuss the activity before students begin the exercise.

## www.rigbyinfoquest.com
## Zone: Plants & Animals
## Link: Sharks

Students can research answers on the site:

1. What is a commonly found fossil?
2. What kind of shark has the longest tail?
3. How do sharks find prey?
4. What are the chances of being attacked by a shark?

## Learning Activities

Students can complete activities on the site:

- Write answers to interview questions about a discovery of a new species.
- Read and interpret the graphs showing shark attack statistics.

What is a commonly found fossil?
Visit www.rigbyinfoquest.com
for more about SHARKS.

# Ocean Life

Name _____     Date _____

Draw a line to match the ocean creatures with a fact about them.

| Ocean Creatures | Facts |
|---|---|
| tube worms | include whales, dolphins, and porpoises |
| beluga whales | look like lumps of seaweed |
| whale sharks | live in the dark zone of the ocean |
| angel sharks | use echolocation to find food |
| cetaceans | live in the twilight zone of the ocean |
| sardines | most have a spiked tail |
| rays | have eyes atop their heads |
| lantern fish | live in the deepest ocean level |
| tassled wobbegong sharks | are the highest worldwide catch yearly |
| herrings, sardines, and anchovies | are the gentle giants of the shark family |

# Nonfiction Assessment Record

**Book Title:** *Giants of the Deep*

Student _____     Date _____

| | | |
|---|---|---|
| Say, *Read pages 6 and 7 silently.* Ask, *What are two natural dangers facing ocean ships?* | Was the student able to recall at least two natural dangers? (Learning Outcome 1) | ☐ |
| Say, *Read pages 8 through 11 silently.* Ask, *What is one similarity and one difference between cetaceans and fish?* | Was the student able to specify one similarity and one difference? (Critical Thinking 1) | ☐ |
| Ask, *How do beluga whales find their food?* | Did the student say "echolocation"? (Purpose for Reading 1) | ☐ |
| Say, *Read pages 15 through 18 silently.* Ask, *Why are there very few creatures in ocean trenches?* | Did the student understand the hostile nature of the environment? (Purpose for Reading 3) | ☐ |
| Say, *Read pages 20 through 23 silently.* Ask, *What do sharks in any particular order have in common?* | Did the student mention gills, fins, snout shape, and/or behavior? (Purpose for Reading 2) | ☐ |
| Ask, *What is one reason sharks are very successful predators?* | Could the student give at least one reason? (Learning Outcome 2) | ☐ |
| Say, *Read pages 26 through 29 silently.* Ask, *Do you think people should be able to hunt whales? Why/Why not?* | Was the student able to form and justify an opinion? (Critical Thinking 2) | ☐ |
| Ask, *What are two ways some countries are trying to preserve the oceans?* | Was the student able to recall at least two ways? (Learning Outcome 3) | ☐ |

# Student Book Notes—*Monuments and Mummies*

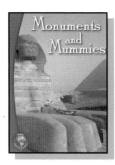

## Synopsis

*Monuments and Mummies* presents a fascinating view of life in ancient Egypt. The book highlights the role of the pharaohs, the amazing pyramids, and the technology used in the embalming of mummies. There are also sections about art, hieroglyphics, and the preservation of artifacts.

## Vocabulary Development
*canopic jars, civilization, demotic script, dynasty, Egyptologist, embalmer, excavation, hieroglyphs, natron, pharaoh, sarcophagi*

### Challenges in the Text
historical perspective

### Cross-Curricular Connections
social studies; art

## Learning Outcomes

Students will:

1. recall the conditions in the Nile Valley that helped the establishment of civilization there.
2. display an understanding of the reasons why the pyramids were constructed.
3. explain the importance of the Rosetta Stone in deciphering hieroglyphics.

## For Independent Readers

Provide these questions before students read the text:

- Why did so many ancient civilizations grow around rivers?
- How were the pyramids built?
- What are some of the ancient Egyptian superstitions?
- Why is the Aswan Dam important?

## Visual Elements

Students have the opportunity to:

1. gain information from a variety of diagrams and photographs.
2. read and interpret a map with labels.
3. view cartoon-style procedural text.
4. view double-page spreads.

## Purposes for Reading

Possible choices include:

1. to learn about the lives and roles of the pharaohs.
2. to learn about some of the ancient Egyptian monuments.
3. to learn about how and why some ancient Egyptians were mummified.

## Critical Thinking

Students have the opportunity to:

1. compare and contrast the lives of the rich and poor in ancient Egypt.
2. interpret and form generalizations from a pyramid diagram of Egyptian society.
3. summarize information as a chart.

## Special Features

- Read "Time Link" and discover where the Greeks and Romans liked to sightsee.
- How well were the pyramids made? Check out "Techtalk" for the answer.
- Were mummies mistreated? Read "What's Your Opinion?" and decide.
- Can you walk like an Egyptian? Try it out through "Fact Finder."

## Guiding Learning

### Before Reading

Hand out copies of Thinking Activity Master 9. Discuss the activity and have students begin to fill in the first two columns of the KWL chart. Students should continue to fill in these columns as they read the book.

### During Reading

Key text to guide:

**Pages 4–5:** Share read these pages. Then discuss both the developments in Upper and Lower Egypt and then the favorable conditions that paved the way for the development of civilization. Help students locate text references on the map.

**Pages 6–9:** Say, *Read to the end of page 9 to find out who the pharaohs were and how they ruled.* When students have finished, discuss what they have found. Highlight and talk about the social class pyramid on page 9.

**Pages 10–11:** Have students read these pages independently. Then challenge them to compare and contrast the lives of the rich and the poor.

**Pages 12–15:** Ask, *Who built the pyramids and why?* Have students offer their ideas and then read these pages independently. Discuss what students have found out and highlight the amazing precision involved in the construction of the pyramids.

**Pages 16–19:** Have students read these pages independently. Then discuss the reasons bodies were mummified and the techniques involved. Challenge students to form and justify opinions about the removal of mummies.

**Pages 20–25:** Share read and discuss pages 20 and 21. Help students understand the tomb diagram. Then have students read independently to the end of page 25. Discuss hieroglyphs and the importance of the Rosetta Stone in deciphering the script.

**Pages 26–27:** Ask, *What would be some of the unique difficulties in Egypt for people trying to preserve tombs and monuments?* Give students time to consider and discuss this, and then have them read these pages. Talk about the importance of the Aswan Dam and the care taken to preserve monuments and temples.

### After Reading

Responding: If necessary, explain how to use the grid framework on pages 28 and 29. Then invite students to follow the instructions and complete the maze.

## Thinking Activity Master 9
### KWL Chart: Summarizing Information

Have individual students share what they have recorded on their KWL charts to date. Then have them complete the final column. Discuss the range of resources that are available, including the Siteseeing site, for answering any remaining questions.

## www.rigbyinfoquest.com
### Zone: Past & Future
### Link: Ancient Egypt

Students can research answers on the site:

1. How did ancient Egyptian people use the River Nile?
2. How did people celebrate in ancient Egypt?
3. Who was Cleopatra?

### Learning Activities

Students can complete activities on the site:

- Take your chances in the ancient Egyptian maze and collect artifacts for a museum.
- Decode the secret message on the ancient Eyptian tablet.

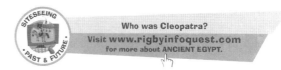

Who was Cleopatra?
Visit www.rigbyinfoquest.com
for more about ANCIENT EGYPT.

# KWL Chart

Name _____     Date _____

Fill in this KWL chart before, during, and after you read *Monuments and Mummies*.

| What I **Know** About Ancient Egypt | What I **Want** to Know About Ancient Egypt | What I **Learned** About Ancient Egypt |
|---|---|---|
| | | |

# Nonfiction Assessment Record

**Book Title:** *Monuments and Mummies*

Student _____     Date _____

| | |
|---|---|
| Say, *Read pages 4 and 5 silently.*<br>Ask, *Why was it possible for civilization to grow in ancient Egypt?* | Did the student understand the importance of the River Nile?<br>(Learning Outcome 1) ☐ |
| Say, *Read pages 6 through 9 silently.*<br>Ask, *Why did the Egyptian people worship the pharaohs?* | Did the student state that pharaohs were believed to be kings of the gods?<br>(Purpose for Reading 1) ☐ |
| Say, *Look at the pyramid on page 9.*<br>Ask, *What does this pyramid tell you about the peasants?* | Was the student able to form an appropriate generalization?<br>(Critical Thinking 2) ☐ |
| Say, *Read pages 10 and 11 silently.*<br>Ask, *How were the lives of the rich and the poor people different?* | Was the student able to specify at least one main difference?<br>(Critical Thinking 1) ☐ |
| Say, *Read pages 12 through 15 silently.*<br>Ask, *What was the main reason the pyramids were built?* | Did the student answer for a display of power or a place of burial?<br>(Learning Outcome 2) ☐ |
| Ask, *Why do many people believe the building of the pyramids was very special?* | Did the student understand that the precision involved before high-tech tools was an amazing feat?<br>(Purpose for Reading 2) ☐ |
| Say, *Read pages 16 and 17 silently.*<br>Ask, *Why did ancient Egyptians mummify people?* | Did the student indicate preparation for an after-life?<br>(Purpose for Reading 3) ☐ |
| Say, *Read pages 22 and 23 silently.*<br>Ask, *Why was the discovery of the Rosetta Stone very important?* | Did the student understand that it was the key to deciphering Egyptian writing? (Learning Outcome 3) ☐ |

# Student Book Notes—*Music, Music, Music!*

### Synopsis

*Music, Music, Music!* Features a variety of musical styles that have been popular throughout the ages. The book highlights musical instruments and presents profiles of some of the past and present's most famous musicians.

## Learning Outcomes

Students will:

1. display an understanding of folk music's significance.
2. be able to describe the influence of electronic instrumentation.
3. explain the importance of The Beatles in forever changing pop music.

## For Independent Readers

Provide these questions before students read the text:

• Why is music popular throughout the world?
• How has video changed popular music?
• What is blues music and where did it originate?
• What is a harpsichord?

## Visual Elements

Students have the opportunity to:

1. view captioned illustrations.
2. read text in scrapbook format.
3. interpret a range of photographs and illustrations.
4. view photographs with labels.

## Purposes for Reading

Possible choices include:

1. to learn about some musical styles.
2. to learn more about a variety of musical instruments.
3. to learn about different ways of constructing an index.

## Critical Thinking

Students have the opportunity to:

1. form generalizations about the cultural importance of music.
2. compare and contrast musical styles.
3. collect, organize, and summarize information about musicians.

## Special Features

• Read "In Focus" and discover how music is made using only household items.
• Check out the "Profile" about an incredible hearing-impaired musician.
• "My Diary" outlines one singer's path to success.

# Guiding Learning

## Before Reading

Read the title to students. Ask, *Why do people throughout the world love to listen to music and create it? What is similar about music around the world?* Have students discuss and justify their responses.

## During Reading

Key text to guide:

**Pages 4–5:** Have students read these pages independently. Then have students recall the many purposes that music serves throughout the world.

**Pages 6–11:** Ask, *How are classical, pop, and folk music similar? How are they different?* Give students time to respond and then have them read independently to the end of page 11. (Share read with students needing support.) When students have finished, discuss what they have read. Challenge them to state some of the features of folk music.

**Pages 12–25:** Read pages 12 and 13 to students. Help them understand the similarities and differences in each class of instrument. Then have students read pages 14 and 15. Comment on how stringed instruments produce sound and about the range of stringed instruments. Continue having students read each double-page spread, in a similar way, to the end of page 25. When students have finished, reread any sections of text the students may have found difficult. Discuss the importance of electronics in changing how we play and listen to music.

**Pages 26–27:** Ask, *How do musicians know what to play? Do they just learn it by heart or do they use some other method?* Invite responses from students and then have them read independently to the end of page 27. Discuss the importance of notation, especially when different instruments are being played.

**Pages 28–29:** Have students read these pages independently. Then highlight the importance of practice and perseverance in the pursuit of personal goals.

**Pages 31**: Discuss the way the index has been organized and how it may be different from other indexes familiar to students. Ask, *Why do you think the author decided to use this form of index?*

## After Reading

Responding: Have students use the index to find and reread information about one of the composers or musicians. Ask, *What was the person's main contribution to music?*

# Thinking Activity Master 10
## Now and Then: Organizing and Summarizing Information

Have students gather and organize information about their and a parent or caregiver's favorite music.

# www.rigbyinfoquest.com
## Zone: Art & Entertainment
## Link: Music

Students can research answers on the site:

1. How can sound be seen?
2. Is the human voice an instrument?
3. How does a portable personal stereo work?
4. How does a compact disc make music?

## Learning Activities

Students can complete activities on the site:

- Write instructions for making a musical shaker.
- Choose your favorite musician and write a profile.

# Now and Then

Name _____     Date _____

Interview one of your parents or caregivers about musical tastes. Write replies to compare and contrast with your own preferences.

| My Favorite | My Parent's Favorite |
|---|---|
| Name of Performer or Group | Name of Performer or Group |
| Type of Music | Type of Music |
| Description of Performer or Group | Description of Performer or Group |
| Favorite Songs Performed | Favorite Songs Performed |
| Why Liked | Why Liked |

# Nonfiction Assessment Record

**Book Title:** *Music, Music, Music!*

Student _____ Date _____

| | |
|---|---|
| Say, *Read pages 4 and 5 silently.* Ask, *Why is music very important to different cultures?* | Was the student able to form an appropriate generalization? (Critical Thinking 1) ☐ |
| Say, *Read pages 6 through 9 silently.* Ask, *How are pop music and classical music similar and different?* | Was the student able to specify at least one similarity and one difference? (Critical Thinking 2) ☐ |
| Ask, *How did The Beatles forever change popular music?* | Did the student understand the worldwide influence of the group's music? (Learning Outcome 3) ☐ |
| Say, *Read pages 10 and 11 silently.* Ask, *Why is folk music important to many people?* | Did the student display an understanding of the timeless nature of folk music? (Learning Outcome 1) ☐ |
| Say, *Read pages 24 and 25 silently.* Ask, *How has the development of electronic instruments changed music?* | Was the student able to summarize some of the changes? (Learning Outcome 2) ☐ |
| Say, *Look at the index on page 31.* Ask, *Why do you think the author constructed the index in this way?* | Did the student understand that the content of the book fit well into two sections? (Purpose for Reading 3) ☐ |
| Ask, *Which music styles from the book have stood the text of time?* | Did the student state "classical" and/or "folk" or a similar appropriate response? (Purpose for Reading 1) ☐ |
| Say, *Choose one instrument from the book and tell me how it produces sound.* | Was the student able to recall an instrument and explain how it produces sound? (Purpose for Reading 2) ☐ |

# Student Book Notes—*On the Move*

### Synopsis
*On the Move* explores the different forms of energy and how forces use that energy to push or pull an object. The book highlights the forces of nature, how they combine, and how people have used their understanding of forces to construct simple and compound machines.

### Vocabulary Development
*air resistance, atom, buoyancy, drag, energy, equilibrium, force, kinetic, lubricant, physicist, pulley, streamlined, radiant, resultant, thermodynamics*

### Challenges in the Text
technical language; procedural text

### Cross-Curricular Connections
physical science; technology

### Learning Outcomes
Students will:
1. be able to specify the relationship between force and energy.
2. explain the differences between potential and kinetic energy.
3. display an understanding of simple machines.

### For Independent Readers
Provide these questions before students read the text:
- Energy can neither be created nor destroyed. What does this mean?
- What is energy transformation?
- What is responsible for the majority of our energy waste?
- What is a renewable energy source?

### Visual Elements
Students have the opportunity to:
1. gain information from a flow diagram.
2. read labeled diagrams.
3. read bulleted text.
4. interpret sequential captions.

### Purposes for Reading
Possible choices include:
1. to learn about some forms of energy.
2. to learn about the ways energy is consumed.
3. to learn about the different forces in nature.

### Critical Thinking
Students have the opportunity to:
1. form and justify opinions about sources of power.
2. sequence events in an example of energy transformation.
3. locate and match information about simple machines.

### Special Features
- "Profile" highlights a man for whom a unit of energy was named.
- Do we use too much electricity? "What's Your Opinion?" lets you have your say.
- Check out "Try This!" and make your own simple machine.
- "Techtalk" explains how an automobile engine works.

## Guiding Learning

### Before Reading

Have students turn to the index. Ask, *What is this book mainly about?* (energy and forces) *How do you know?* Discuss the prominence of these two entries in the table of contents and index.

### During Reading

Key text to guide:

**Pages 4–5:** Ask, *Why do things move? Why don't they just stay still?* Then have students read these pages independently. Discuss the natures of force and energy and how they are related.

**Pages 6–11:** Say, *Read to the end of page 11 to find out about the different forms of energy and how they are transformed from one form into another.* (Share read with students needing support.) When students have finished, discuss the examples of energy transformation, concentrating on potential and kinetic energy. Then invite students to form and justify opinions on energy sources and our dependence on electricity.

**Pages 12–15:** Ask, *How does the food we eat provide the energy we need?* Then have students read these pages independently. Ensure that they understand the different kinds of energy transformations taking place.

**Pages 16–21:** Say, *Gravity and friction are two of nature's main forces. Read to the end of page 21 to find out how each force works and how they interact.* When students have finished, reread pages 20 and 21 with them and then discuss the interaction of forces acting on the airplane.

**Pages 22–23:** Have students read the body text on these pages. Discuss the simple machines and next invite students to think of other examples. If possible, have students make their own block and tackle.

**Pages 24–25:** Have students read the body text on these pages. Then read the "Techtalk" section aloud. Highlight the fact that examples of most simple machines can be found in the internal combustion engine.

**Pages 26–27:** Read through the procedural text with students and, if appropriate, have them construct the magic box.

**Pages 28–29:** Ask, *Do the forces of nature remain the same in space?* Have students read these pages and discuss the effects of zero gravity on people and materials.

### After Reading

Responding: Reread pages 8 and 9. Challenge students to think of other everyday examples of energy transformation.

## Thinking Activity Master 11
### Simple Machines: Locating and Matching Information

Read through the directions with students. Then have them complete the activity. When they have finished, invite them to share and compare their responses.

## www.rigbyinfoquest.com
### Zone: Science & Technology
### Link: Physics

Students can research answers on the site:

1. Why does the moon circle Earth?
2. Does gravity exist inside a spacecraft?
3. Why does a feather fall slowly?
4. What is terminal velocity?
5. Why does a basketball bounce?
6. Why can you balance on a moving bicycle but not on a stationary one?

### Learning Activities

Students can complete activities on the site:

- Write a story about time travel.
- Answer the questions to make the hot-air balloon fly.

Does gravity exist inside a spacecraft?
Visit www.rigbyinfoquest.com
for more about PHYSICS.

# Simple Machines

Name _____    Date _____

1. Write each of the following items under the heading of the simple machine it uses.
   Then think of one more item to write under each heading.
2. Match each simple machine with its description.

*bicycle, zipper, straight staircase, teeter-totter, flagpole,*
*spiral staircase, scissors, wagon, axe, crane, boat propeller,*
*parking ramp, knife, bolt, window blinds, bottle opener*

**Levers**                **Wedges**                **Wheels**




**Pulleys**               **Screws**                **Ramps**




used to split an object                                    lever
or stop it from moving

has a small surface area that                              ramp
overcomes the force of friction

moves heavy objects without                                wedge
lifting straight up

uses rotational force to push                              wheel
in a different direction

changes force direction to                                 screw
help overcome gravity

distributes a load to help                                 pulley
overcome gravity

# Nonfiction Assessment Record

**Book Title:** *On the Move*

Student _____     Date _____

| | | |
|---|---|---|
| Say, *Read pages 4 and 5 silently.* Ask, *What causes a force to work on an object?* | Did the student say "energy"? (Learning Outcome 1) | ☐ |
| Say, *Read pages 6 and 7 silently.* Ask, *What are three ways that electrical energy can be generated?* | Was the student able to specify at least three different types of generation? (Purpose for Reading 1) | ☐ |
| Say, *Read pages 8 and 9 silently.* Ask, *Can you explain the steps that transform the energy in a candle?* | Was the student able to appropriately sequence the events? (Critical Thinking 2) | ☐ |
| Ask, *Do you think nuclear power plants are a good idea? Why/Why not?* | Was the student able to form and justify an opinion? (Critical Thinking 1) | ☐ |
| Say, *Read pages 10 and 11 silently.* Ask, *What is the difference between kinetic and potential energy?* | Did the student display an understanding of the difference? (Learning Outcome 2) | ☐ |
| Say, *Read pages 12 through 15 silently.* Ask, *What are two types of energy transformed from food by our bodies?* | Did the student specify at least two different kinds of energy? (Purpose for Reading 2) | ☐ |
| Say, *Read pages 16 through 19 silently.* Ask, *What are two forces that help us slow down when we are running?* | Did the student say "gravity" and "friction"? (Purpose for Reading 3) | ☐ |
| Say, *Read pages 22 and 23 silently.* Ask, *What main force do pulleys and levers help overcome?* | Did the student say "gravity"? (Learning Outcome 3) | ☐ |

# Student Book Notes—*Our Inside Story*

## Synopsis

*Our Inside Story* explains how some of the main systems in our bodies work. It highlights the advances made in technology that allow for more comprehensive diagnosis and treatment of ailments. A section on the use of prosthetics is included.

**Vocabulary Development**

*anatomy, blood platelet, cadaver, circulatory system, conscious, cosmetic, diagnosis, dominant, hallucinate, insomnia, neuron, physiology, prosthesis, recessive, skeletal, subconscious, trait*

**Challenges in the Text**
vocabulary

**Cross-Curricular Connections**
life science; technology; health

## Learning Outcomes

Students will:

1. explain how personal traits are determined.
2. recall the main components of the nervous system.
3. display an understanding of what happens to the brain as we sleep.

## For Independent Readers

Provide these questions before students read the text:

- What causes allergies?
- Why do we have specific hair and eye colors?
- What is the difference between fraternal and identical twins?
- What is the main benefit of pain?

## Visual Elements

Students have the opportunity to:

1. gain information from a variety of diagrams and photographs.
2. read diagrams with labels.
3. read information in game form.
4. view cross sections.

## Purposes for Reading

Possible choices include:

1. to learn about nature and nurture.
2. to learn about some advances in physiology and anatomy.
3. to learn about the ways some of our body systems function.

## Critical Thinking

Students have the opportunity to:

1. summarize the functions of the immune system.
2. form and justify opinions about nature versus nurture.
3. locate and record important information about systems in the body.

## Special Features

- "In Focus" features a doctor who prescribed strange forms of treatment.
- Why are some people good at math? Read "What's your Opinion?" and think.
- How many years of our lives do we sleep? "Fast Facts" has the answer.

# Guiding Learning

## Before Reading

Ask, *Why do some people have blue eyes while others have brown?* Have students recall the eye color of their parents. Discuss other traits that are linked to inheritance.

## During Reading

Key text to guide:

**Pages 4–7:** Share read these pages. Discuss the advances in technology that have allowed better diagnosis and treatment. Ask, *How do you think medical technology will affect your adult life?*

**Pages 8–11:** Have students read these pages independently. Help students understand the differences between nature and nurture. Reread the "What's Your Opinion?" section and invite students to form and justify opinions about the acquisition of mathematical skills.

**Pages 12–13:** Ask, *Why do we feel pain when we accidentally hurt ourselves?* Have students read these pages independently and then discuss their understanding of the nervous system. Ensure that students understand the "How Nerves Work" diagram.

**Pages 14–15:** Ask, *What are the main functions of the brain?* Have students discuss their responses and then share read these pages. Talk about how the two halves of the brain function.

**Pages 16–17:** Ask, *Why is sleep very important?* Have students read these pages independently and then highlight the differences between the activities of the conscious and unconscious brain. Help students understand REM sleep.

**Pages 18–19:** Say, *Read to the end of page 19 to find out what the immune system does.* When students have finished, discuss the benefits and downside of this system.

**Pages 20–21:** See "After Reading."

**Pages 22–27:** Say, *The next six pages tell us about our lungs, muscles, and bones. Read to the end of page 27 to find out the importance of each system and how each works.* (Share read with students needing further support.) Have students share what they have learned. Reread any text sections that students may have found challenging.

**Pages 28–29:** Ask, *Which body part can now be replaced?* Then have students read these pages independently and discuss how technology has made a difference.

## After Reading

Responding: Provide dice or spinners and have students complete the "Go with the Flow" activity on pages 20 and 21.

# Thinking Activity Master 12
## The Inside Story: Locating and Recording Important Information

Review how the contents page, glossary, and index can be used to locate specific facts before students complete the activity.

# www.rigbyinfoquest.com
## Zone: Science & Technology
## Link: Illness

Students can research answers on the site:
1. Where is blood made?
2. What are some bone marrow illnesses?
3. Why are sick people often feverish?
4. What other natural defenses does the body have?
5. What is immunization?
6. What was the first illness prevented by immunization?

## Learning Activities

Students can complete activities on the site:
- Take a journey through the bloodstream by playing "Go with the Flow."
- Make a gene tree showing dominant and recessive genes.

Why are sick people often feverish?
Visit www.rigbyinfoquest.com
for more about ILLNESS.

# Our Inside Story

Name _____     Date _____

Use the index, glossary, and contents page to find information and complete the following chart.

| Body Part | Main Function(s) | Keeping Healthy | Interesting Fact(s) |
|---|---|---|---|
| Immune System | Defends the body from poisons and germs | Keep wounds clean and covered. | Allergies are caused by the immune system being too ready to defend. |
| Brain | | | |
| Lungs | | | |
| Nervous System | | | |
| Skin | | | |
| Muscles | | | |
| Bones | | | |

© 2004 RIGBY—*RIGBY INFOQUEST*

# Nonfiction Assessment Record

**Book Title:** *Our Inside Story*

Student _____    Date _____

| | | |
|---|---|---|
| Say, *Read pages 6 and 7 silently.* Ask, *How has technology helped in dealing with some diseases?* | Did the student mention improved diagnosis and/or treatment? (Purpose for Reading 2) | ☐ |
| Say, *Read pages 8 through 11 silently.* Ask, *How are personal traits such as eye color determined?* | Did the student understand the function of genes in determining personal traits? (Learning Outcome 1) | ☐ |
| Ask, *What is the difference between nature and nurture?* | Was the student able to explain the difference? (Purpose for Reading 1) | ☐ |
| Ask, *Do you think anyone can be good at math? Why/Why not?* | Was the student able to form and justify an opinion? (Critical Thinking 2) | ☐ |
| Say, *Read pages 12 and 13 silently.* Ask, *What are the three main parts of the nervous system?* | Was the student able to recall the nerves, brain, and spinal cord? (Learning Outcome 2) | ☐ |
| Say, *Read pages 16 and 17 silently.* Ask, *What happens to your brain when you are asleep?* | Did the student understand that his or her subconscious takes over? (Learning Outcome 3) | ☐ |
| Say, *Read pages 18 and 19 silently.* Ask, *In what ways is the immune system useful and also a problem?* | Was the student able to summarize the benefits and problems of the immune system? (Critical Thinking 1) | ☐ |
| Say, *Thinking of the whole book, choose one system in the body and explain how it works.* | Was the student able to explain how one system in the body works? (Purpose for Reading 3) | ☐ |

# Student Book Notes—*Peace Makers*

### Synopsis

*Peace Makers* highlights the lives of four very different people who contributed to making the world a better place. The text also features the development of the Red Cross and the United Nations, as well as the nonviolent movement in the fight for rights.

### Vocabulary Development

*boycott, concentration camps, constitution, diplomat, discriminate, ethnic, ghetto, humanitarian, massacre, Nazis, neutral, occupy, oppress, pacifist, political prisoner, prejudice, treaty*

### Challenges in the Text

historical perspective; biographical text

### Cross-Curricular Connections

social studies—history

## Learning Outcomes

Students will:

1. display an understanding of the significance of the Nobel Peace Prize.
2. recall ways that ordinary people can make a difference.
3. be able to explain the importance of the United Nations.

## For Independent Readers

Provide these questions before students read the text:

- Who have been famous peace makers?
- Who is the peace maker in your family?
- How can you help make a difference?
- What are different types of discrimination?

## Visual Elements

Students have the opportunity to:

1. interpret a time line.
2. read a map with leadered text.
3. view a variety of historical photographs.
4. view cartoon-style illustrations.

## Purposes for Reading

Possible choices include:

1. to learn about several people who have worked for peace.
2. to learn about the nonviolent fight for human rights.
3. to learn about the development of the modern Red Cross.

## Critical Thinking

Students have the opportunity to:

1. form generalizations about the four featured peace keepers.
2. form and justify opinions about forms of protest.
3. compose, sequence, and summarize information in the form of a profile.

## Special Features

- What kind of war is a civil war? Read "Fast Facts" and discover the answer.
- "In Focus" tells about one of the most horrific events in world history.
- Check out "My Diary" to learn how it feels to be a child caught in the middle of a war.

# Guiding Learning

## Before Reading

Read the title with students. Ask, *How do wars and other conflicts start? Is it possible to avoid them?* Have students discuss and debate their responses to these questions.

## During Reading

Key text to guide:

**Pages 4–5:** Ask, *What is special about people who are able to bring about resolutions to conflict?* Have students discuss their responses and then read these pages independently. When finished, talk about "courage of their convictions" and the importance of the Nobel Peace Prize.

**Pages 6–9:** Have students read these pages independently. Then discuss the concept of apartheid. Ask, *Why do you think Nelson Mandela abandoned his belief in nonviolence? Do you think violence is ever justified? Why/Why not?*

**Pages 10–11:** Read these pages to students. Talk about the ways that nonviolent protests have worked in different parts of the world.

**Pages 12–15:** Say, *Read to the end of page 15. Find out who Clara Barton was and why she was special.* When students have finished, highlight the particular problems facing women and Clara's persistence in making significant change.

**Pages 16–17:** Read these pages to students. Highlight the fact that the Red Cross is important in both times of war and peace.

**Pages 18–21:** Say, *Read to the end of page 21 and find out how one person was responsible for saving the lives of thousands of people.* When students have finished, sensitively discuss the holocaust and how a neutral person was able to save many others.

**Pages 22–23:** Read these pages to students and discuss the various roles of the United Nations.

**Pages 24–27:** Ask, *How could a child possibly influence the peace process?* Then have students read these pages independently. When students have finished, talk about how Zlata's writing has helped inspire other children to try to make a difference.

**Pages 28–29:** Have students read these pages and discuss how ordinary people can make the world a more peaceful place.

## After Reading

Responding: Challenge students to state the similarities and differences among the four main peace makers in the book.

# Thinking Activity Master 13
## Making a Difference: Composing, Sequencing, and Summarizing Information

Discuss people, including family members, who have made a difference in individual students' lives. Read through the worksheet and then have students complete the activity.

# www.rigbyinfoquest.com
## Zone: People & Places
## Link: Peace

Students can research answers on the site:

1. What do paper cranes symbolize?
2. What are some other symbols of peace?
3. When is the International Day of Peace?
4. What is special about Waterton-Glacier Peace Park?

## Learning Activities

Students can complete activities on the site:

• Make a paper crane that symbolizes peace.
• Write about a conflict and how you would settle it.

SITESEEING · PEOPLE & PLACES

What do paper cranes symbolize?
Visit www.rigbyinfoquest.com
for more about PEACE.

# Making a Difference

Name _____ Date _____

Choose a person who has make a significant difference in your life and make a time line about that person's life.

A Time Line of Important Events in _____'s Life

| DATE | EVENT |
|------|-------|
| | |
| | |
| | |
| | |

(Continue on the back if needed.)

The biggest difference this person has made in me is _____

_____

_____

_____

I chose this person because _____

_____

_____

_____

© 2004 RIGBY—RIGBY INFOQUEST

# Nonfiction Assessment Record

**Book Title:** *Peace Makers*

Student _____     Date _____

| | |
|---|---|
| Say, *Read pages 4 and 5 silently.* Ask, *For what is the Nobel Peace Prize awarded?* | Did the student understand that it reflects the largest contribution to world peace? (Learning Outcome 1) ☐ |
| Say, *Read pages 6 and 7 silently.* Ask, *Should Nelson Mandela have abandoned nonviolence? Why/Why not?* | Was the student able to form and justify an appropriate opinion? (Critical Thinking 2) ☐ |
| Say, *Read pages 10 and 11 silently.* Ask, *What do the three accounts on these pages have in common?* | Did the student understand that they all involved nonviolence? (Purpose for Reading 2) ☐ |
| Say, *Read pages 16 and 17 silently.* Ask, *How does the Red Cross help in times of peace?* | Was the student able to recall at least two different ways? (Purpose for Reading 3) ☐ |
| Say, *Read pages 22 and 23 silently.* Ask, *What are some of the important roles of the United Nations?* | Was the student able to specify at least two important roles? (Learning Outcome 3) ☐ |
| Say, *Read pages 28 and 29 silently.* Ask, *How can ordinary people contribute to world peace?* | Was the student able to form an appropriate generalization? (Learning Outcome 2) ☐ |
| Ask, *Which of the four featured peace makers in the book do you most admire? Why?* | Did the student relate the contributions of one peace maker? (Purpose for Reading 1) ☐ |
| Ask, *What main quality did all four featured peace makers possess?* | Did the student recognize the importance of passion or a similar quality? (Critical Thinking 1) ☐ |

# Student Book Notes—*People of the Past*

## Synopsis

*People of the Past* outlines the growth of civilization from early cave life to the rise of the first city-states. The book features the growth of technology that brought about the shift from hunting and gathering to farming, trading, and the development of permanent settlements.

**Vocabulary Development**
*artifact, carbon, city-state, civilization, domestic, handicraft, historian, ice age, prehistoric, surplus, ziggurat*

**Challenges in the Text**
time line; historical perspective

**Cross-Curricular Connections**
social studies

## Learning Outcomes

Students will:
1. understand why researchers believe the earliest people lived in East Africa.
2. be able to state the benefits of trade to early civilizations.
3. recall some of the factors that led to the rise of city-states.

## For Independent Readers

Provide these questions before students read the text:
- From where did the first people come, and how do we know?
- What tools did prehistoric people use?
- Where were the first major settlements located near rivers?
- Why was the control of fire important?

## Visual Elements

Students have the opportunity to:
1. view sequential diagrams.
2. read a time line with captions.
3. interpret a range of photographs and illustrations.
4. view double-page spreads.

## Purposes for Reading

Possible choices include:
1. to learn about how prehistoric people lived.
2. to learn about the movement from hunting and gathering to farming.
3. to learn about daily life in the early city-states.

## Critical Thinking

Students have the opportunity to:
1. form generalizations about the production and control of fire.
2. summarize the changes that took place between 10,000 and 2,500 years ago.
3. compose, sequence, and summarize information in the form of a diary.

## Special Features

- How old are the oldest cave paintings? "Time Link" has the answer.
- "In Focus" describes what life must have been like in a Stone Age village.
- Read "Techtalk" and find out how scientists determine how old an artifact is.

## Guiding Learning

### Before Reading

Read the title to students and invite them to discuss what they know about people in the far past. Ask, *When did people stop living in caves? Where were the first cities located?*

### During Reading

Key text to guide:

**Pages 4–5:** Read these pages to students. Discuss the difficulty of life for early people and how banding together was the first sign of the beginnings of civilization.

**Pages 6–11:** Say, *Read to the end of page 11 and find out what life was like for prehistoric people.* (Share read sections with students needing support.) When students have finished, discuss the use of early tools and the importance in being able to make and control fire.

**Pages 12–13:** Ask, *Where do many scientists believe human life began, and how did it spread?* Have students read these pages independently and respond to the questions. Talk about the climatic conditions that allowed early people to reach North America.

**Pages 14–19:** Ask, *What would be the advantages of farming instead of hunting and gathering?* Give students time to respond and then have them read to the end of page 19. Help students understand that farming created more leisure time and surpluses, which led to the rise of trade.

**Pages 20–21:** Tell students that these two pages summarize development over 7,500 years. Have them read the text and view the illustrations. Challenge students to state why permanent settlements were a natural outcome of this progression.

**Pages 22–27:** Say, *Read to the end of page 27 to find out how and where the first permanent civilizations began.* (Share read with students needing support.) When students have finished, highlight the importance of rivers to farming and transportation, and the contributions made by the Sumerians.

**Pages 28–29:** Read page 28 to students. Then help them read and interpret the time line on page 29. Ask, *What was the earliest civilization? What contributions did ancient China make?*

### After Reading

Responding: Have students discuss what they have learned about the progression from cave life to city-states. Ask, *How do you think civilization will change in the future?*

## Thinking Activity Master 14
### Cave Dweller's Diary: Composing, Sequencing, and Summarizing Information

Review students' experiences of reading or writing diaries. Emphasize the format (chronology, informal language, etc.). Have students use information from the book to write about a day in the life of a cave person.

## www.rigbyinfoquest.com
### Zone: People & Places
### Link: Prehistoric People

Students can research answers on the site:

1. Where is Beringia?
2. Who were the first people in North America?
3. Who were the Cro-Magnon people?
4. Where is Çatal Hüyük?
5. What do anthropologists study?

### Learning Activities

Students can complete activities on the site:

- Write about a cave painting.
- Write clues for the *People of the Past* crossword puzzle.

Who were the first people in North America?
Visit www.rigbyinfoquest.com
for more about PREHISTORIC PEOPLE.

# Cave Dweller's Diary

Name _____     Date _____

Imagining yourself as a prehistoric cave dweller, write about events, thoughts, and feelings at different times of the day.

Time: _____     _____

_____

_____

_____

Time: _____     _____

_____

_____

_____

Time: _____     _____

_____

_____

_____

Time: _____     _____

_____

_____

_____

Time: _____     _____

_____

_____

_____

## Nonfiction Assessment Record

**Book Title:** *People of the Past*

Student _____     Date _____

| | | |
|---|---|---|
| Say, *Read pages 6 through 9 silently.* Ask, *Why were caves important to prehistoric people?* | Did the student understand the importance of warmth and safety? (Purpose for Reading 1) | ☐ |
| Ask, *How did the production and control of fire change the lives of cave people?* | Was the student able to form an appropriate generalization about the use of fire? (Critical Thinking 1) | ☐ |

| | | |
|---|---|---|
| Say, *Read pages 12 and 13 silently.* Ask, *Why do many researchers believe the first humans came from East Africa?* | Did the student understand the significance of archaeological evidence? (Learning Outcome 1) | ☐ |

| | | |
|---|---|---|
| Say, *Read pages 16 and 17 silently.* Ask, *What were two benefits of the rise of farming?* | Was the student able to supply at least two benefits? (Purpose for Reading 2) | ☐ |

| | | |
|---|---|---|
| Say, *Read pages 18 and 19 silently.* Ask, *Why were early trading centers important to people?* | Was the student able to form an appropriate generalization? (Learning Outcome 2) | ☐ |

| | | |
|---|---|---|
| Say, *Read pages 20 and 21 silently.* Ask, *What were the major changes from 10,000 to 2,500 years ago?* | Was the student able to summarize the major changes? (Critical Thinking 2) | ☐ |

| | | |
|---|---|---|
| Say, *Read pages 22 and 23 silently.* Ask, *What were the main reasons for the rise of city-states?* | Was the student able to supply at least two reasons? (Learning Outcome 3) | ☐ |

| | | |
|---|---|---|
| Say, *Read pages 26 and 27 silently.* Ask, *Can you describe life for the average Sumerian family?* | Did the student understand that life was extremely difficult for the average family? (Purpose for Reading 3) | ☐ |

© 2004 Rigby—Rigby InfoQuest

# Student Book Notes—*Rebels and Revolutions*

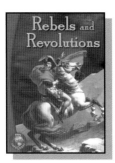

## Synopsis

*Rebels and Revolutions* traces the causes, events, and results of some of the major revolutions throughout history. It highlights the main participants, as well as people who have worked for change in a nonviolent way.

**Vocabulary Development**
*boycott, colonist, Communist Party, democratic, dictatorship, discriminate, equality, frontiersman, liberty, pacifist, segregate*

**Challenges in the Text**
historical perspective; biographies

**Cross-Curricular Connections**
social studies; technology

## Learning Outcomes

Students will:
1. be able to explain the main causes of revolutions.
2. display an understanding of why revolutions continue today.
3. recall how the Technological Revolution is changing people's lives.

## For Independent Readers

Provide these questions before students read the text:
- What causes revolutions?
- Can people make important changes without resorting to violence?
- What are some of the reasons why people choose to protest?
- Can revolutions be avoided? How?

## Visual Elements

Students have the opportunity to:
1. read maps with keys.
2. read a captioned world map.
3. interpret a variety of photographs and illustrations.
4. view double-page spreads.

## Purposes for Reading

Possible choices include:
1. to learn about a range of revolutions throughout history.
2. to learn about the events and outcomes of the French Revolution.
3. to learn about some of the people involved in nonviolent protests.

## Critical Thinking

Students have the opportunity to:
1. form generalizations about revolutions in different parts of the world.
2. summarize the advantages and disadvantages of the Chinese Revolution.
3. locate and organize information about a range of revolutions.

## Special Features

- "My Diary" features a letter from one very brave man in history.
- Find out how East Timor finally won independence. "In Focus" traces the road to freedom for this tiny nation.
- Read "Profile" and find out how one woman managed to gain equal voting rights for others.

## Guiding Learning

### Before Reading

Read the title to students and ask, *What is a revolution? Why do revolutions happen? Are the outcomes always for the best?* Record students' responses for the "After Reading" section.

### During Reading

Key text to guide:

**Pages 4–5:** Read these pages to students. Talk about the conditions that lead to revolutions and how people often view the outcomes differently.

**Pages 6–9:** Say, *Read to the end of page 9 and find the causes and events surrounding different revolutions around the world.* (Share read with students needing support.) When students have finished, challenge them to state some ways these revolutions were similar.

**Pages 10–13:** Have students read these pages independently. Then reread this section together, highlighting the causes, main events, and final outcomes of the French Revolution.

**Pages 14–15:** Say, *Read to the end of page 15 to find out about the revolution in Texas.* When students have finished, discuss the bravery and willpower displayed by the men who defended the Alamo.

**Pages 16–19:** Say, *Read to the end of page 19 to find out some of the similarities and differences between the Chinese and French revolutions.* Then review this section and highlight the similarities in pre-revolution conditions and the rise of particularly strong leaders.

**Pages 20–23:** Say, *Revolutions are not just a thing of the past. Read to the end of page 23 and find out about current conditions.* When students have finished, challenge them to recall some of the conditions that currently lead to unrest.

**Pages 24–27:** Say, *Not all revolutions involve violence. Read to the end of page 27 and find out about people who worked for change in nonviolent ways.* When students have finished, review the accomplishments of these special people.

**Pages 28–29:** Have students read these pages independently and discuss some effects of the ongoing Technological Revolution.

### After Reading

Responding: Reread students' responses during the "Before Reading" session. Challenge the group to review these in light of what they have now read.

## Thinking Activity Master 15

### Revolution Review: Locating and Organizing Information

Review how to use text organizers such as the index and contents pages to help locate appropriate information. Then read through the worksheet with students before having them complete the activity. If necessary, complete the first row as a model.

## www.rigbyinfoquest.com

**Zone: People & Places**

**Link: Revolutions**

Students can research answers on the site:

1. What caused the U.S. Civil War?
2. Who was the last Russian czar?
3. Why was Mahatma Gandhi famous?

### Learning Activities

Students can complete activities on the site:

- Complete a time line.
- Choose a revolution and make a fact web about it.

What caused the U.S. Civil War?
Visit www.rigbyinfoquest.com
for more about REVOLUTIONS.

# Revolution Review

Name _____ Date _____

Use the index and contents pages of *Rebels and Revolutions* to list information about these conflicts.

| Conflict | Causes | Events | Long-Term Effects | Important People |
|---|---|---|---|---|
| Chinese Revolution | | | | |
| Battle of the Alamo | | | | |
| French Revolution | | | | |
| East Timor Conflict | | | | |

# Nonfiction Assessment Record

**Book Title:** *Rebels and Revolutions*

Student _____     Date _____

| | |
|---|---|
| Say, *Read pages 4 and 5 silently.* Ask, *What are some main causes of revolutions?* | Was the student able to state at least two different causes or pre-conditions? (Learning Outcome 1) ☐ |
| Say, *Read pages 8 and 9 silently.* Ask, *What was similar about revolutions in Africa and South America?* | Did the student display an understanding of the effects of colonialism? (Critical Thinking 1) ☐ |
| Say, *Read pages 10 through 13 silently.* Ask, *How did Napoleon forever change life in Europe?* | Did the student indicate that the seeds of democracy had now been sown? (Purpose for Reading 2) ☐ |
| Say, *Read pages 16 through 19 silently.* Ask, *What were the advantages and disadvantages of the Chinese Revolution?* | Was the student able to state at least one advantage and one disadvantage? (Critical Thinking 2) ☐ |
| Say, *Read pages 20 and 21 silently.* Ask, *Why do revolutions still happen in modern times?* | Was the student able to form an appropriate generalization? (Learning Outcome 2) ☐ |
| Say, *Read pages 26 and 27 silently.* Ask, *How was Martin Luther King's protest different from many other types of protest?* | Did the student understand that this form of protest was nonviolent? (Purpose for Reading 3) ☐ |
| Say, *Read pages 28 and 29 silently.* Ask, *How is the Technological Revolution changing people's lives?* | Did the student display an understanding of the impact of technology? (Learning Outcome 3) ☐ |
| Say, *Choose one revolution from the book.* Ask, *What were the pre-conditions and the outcomes of that revolution?* | Was the student able to locate and recall the appropriate information? (Purpose for Reading 1) ☐ |

# Student Book Notes—*Secrets of the Sky*

## Synopsis

*Secrets of the Sky* explores some mysteries of space, highlighting the development of telescopes and satellite technology. The book includes a time line of our ventures into space to date.

## Vocabulary Development

*astronomer, Big Bang theory, black hole, eclipse, electromagnetic spectrum, galaxy, gravity, light-year, nebula, orbit, simulator, universe*

### Challenges in the Text

scientific language

### Cross-Curricular Connections

earth science; history

## Learning Outcomes

Students will:

1. be able to explain why the sun is highly important to us.
2. display an understanding of the importance of the Hubble Telescope.
3. describe the differences between meteoroids and meteorites.

## For Independent Readers

Provide these questions before students read the text:

- Why is the possible discovery of water on Mars important?
- How large is the Milky Way?
- What are the qualities necessary to be a successful astronaut?
- How powerful were the first telescopes?

## Visual Elements

Students have the opportunity to:

1. view sequential diagrams.
2. read diagrams with labels.
3. view photographs and illustrations.
4. read illustration captions.

## Purposes for Reading

Possible choices include:

1. to learn about the development of telescopes.
2. to learn more about the main objects in the universe.
3. to learn about the history of the exploration of space.

## Critical Thinking

Students have the opportunity to:

1. summarize the events included in the Big Bang theory.
2. form and justify an opinion about the existence of extraterrestrial life.
3. recognize and summarize important information in the form of a newspaper article.

## Special Features

- Is there a new planet in the solar system? Read "In the News" and find out.
- Not all telescopes are used to see things. "Techtalk" explains why.
- Read "In Focus" and find out about Stephen Hawking's theory of black holes.

## Guiding Learning

### Before Reading

Have students view the cover and title page. Ask, *When we look at the night sky, what are we really seeing?* Help them understand that what is seen is really a picture of the past.

### During Reading

Key text to guide:

**Pages 4–5:** Ask, *Why are people fascinated with what lies beyond the Earth?* Share read and discuss the forms of expression.

**Pages 6–7:** Have students read these pages independently. Reread the star life cycle and help students understand the chronology.

**Pages 8–9:** Say, *Read to the end of page 9 and find out how people first started to study the solar system.* When students finish, discuss the importance of Galileo's work.

**Pages 10–11:** Have students read page 10 and then read page 11 to them. Discuss how technology is helping astronomers discover new objects.

**Pages 12–13:** Ask, *How big is the universe, and how do scientists think it began?* Have students read these pages and then discuss the events in the Big Bang theory.

**Pages 14–18:** Ask, *How have telescopes changed since Galileo's time?* Have students read these pages independently. (Share read with students needing support.) Then discuss the development of the telescope. Reread the time line, highlighting the relatively short period during which space has been explored.

**Page 19:** Read page 19 to students. Have them form and justify opinions about the existence of extraterrestrial life.

**Pages 20–21:** Share read these pages. Discuss the importance of the Hubble Telescope in allowing us to see distant objects with greater clarity.

**Pages 22–25:** Say, *There are other objects besides planets and moons in our solar system. Read to the end of page 25 to find out what these are.* When students have finished, discuss the differences between meteoroids and meteorites.

**Pages 26–29:** Have students read independently. Discuss the experiences of Roberta Bondar and the young people at space camp.

### After Reading

Responding: Have students choose an astronomer from the index, reread appropriately, and comment on the person's contributions to knowledge or exploration.

## Thinking Activity Master 16
### Late-Breaking News: Recognizing and Summarizing Important Information

Discuss devices such as headlines, columns, photographs, and direct quotes that are used in newspaper articles. Then have students use what they've read to write an article about the discovery of a new planet or a signal from space.

## www.rigbyinfoquest.com
### Zone: Science & Technology
### Link: Outer Space

Students can research answers on the site:

1. What is a black hole?
2. Why can't people see black holes?
3. How big is the Milky Way galaxy?
4. Are all galaxies the same?
5. How did Earth get its moon?
6. Why does the moon have an uneven surface?

### Learning Activities

Students can complete activities on the site:

- Do you know why stars twinkle? Try this experiment to find out.
- Navigate your way on the moon to answer a question about its night.

Why can't people see black holes?
Visit www.rigbyinfoquest.com
for more about OUTER SPACE.

# Late-Breaking News

Name _____     Date _____

1. Choose the topic of either the discovery of a new planet or a signal from space. Think of an exciting headline and write the headline on the line.
2. Write your article in the two long column boxes. Use the small box at the bottom to sketch the photograph you'd like to include.

_____

# Nonfiction Assessment Record

**Book Title:** *Secrets of the Sky*

Student _____     Date _____

| | | |
|---|---|---|
| Say, *Read pages 6 and 7 silently.* Ask, *What are two reasons the sun is very important to Earth?* | Did the student indicate climate and life support or similar concepts? (Learning Outcome 1) | ☐ |
| Say, *Read pages 8 and 9 silently.* Ask, *What theory did Galileo and his telescope help to prove?* | Did the student say that the Earth orbits the sun or a similar wording of the concept? (Purpose for Reading 1) | ☐ |
| Say, *Read pages 12 and 13 silently.* Ask, *Can you list the following from largest to smallest: galaxy, Earth, universe, solar system?* | Was the student able to list the four objects in the correct order? (Purpose for Reading 2) | ☐ |
| Ask, *What were the main events involved in the Big Bang theory?* | Was the student able to recall the main events? (Critical Thinking 1) | ☐ |
| Say, *Read pages 16 through 19 silently.* Ask, *In what year did the first person walk on the moon?* | Did the student say 1969? (Purpose for Reading 3) | ☐ |
| Ask, *Do you think that life exists on planets other than Earth? Why/Why not?* | Did the student form and justify an opinion? (Critical Thinking 2) | ☐ |
| Say, *Read pages 20 and 21 silently.* Ask, *Why is the Hubble Telescope important to our understanding of outer space?* | Did the student understand the importance in terms of clarity and depth? (Learning Outcome 2) | ☐ |
| Say, *Read pages 22 and 23 silently.* Ask, *What is the main difference between meteoroids and meteorites?* | Did the student understand that when meteoroids hit the Earth they are called meteorites? (Learning Outcome 3) | ☐ |

# Student Book Notes—*Shifting Perspectives*

## Synopsis

*Shifting Perspectives* presents a detailed look at how the human eye functions. It includes sections on eye problems and the use of technology in correcting them. The book also includes some optical illusions that illustrate how the brain interprets visual information.

**Vocabulary Development**
*electromagnetic, illusion, optic, paradox, peripheral, stereotype*
**Challenges in the Text**
technical vocabulary
**Cross-Curricular Connections**
life science; technology

## Learning Outcomes

Students will:

1. display an understanding of difficulties associated with sight.
2. be able to state some of the contributions made by Helen Keller.
3. explain the role of perspective in interpreting what we see.

## For Independent Readers

Provide these questions before students read the text:

- Which of the five senses do you think is the most important?
- Why are some people color-blind?
- What is a mirage? What causes a mirage?
- What is Braille, and how do people use it to read and write?

## Visual Elements

Students have the opportunity to:

1. view and interpret optical illusions.
2. read a diagram with labels.
3. view a variety of photographs and illustrations.

## Purposes for Reading

Possible choices include:

1. to learn about some developments in improving eye conditions.
2. to learn how the brain functions as the eye perceives stimuli.
3. to learn how our perceptions of events can change over time.

## Critical Thinking

Students have the opportunity to:

1. sequence events that occur during the act of seeing an object.
2. form and justify opinions about stereotypes based on physical appearance.
3. locate, check, and organize information in the form of a glossary.

## Special Features

- Helen Keller was a truly remarkable person. Read her story in "Profile."
- How do you surf airwaves? Turn to "In Focus" and find out.
- Check out some amazing eye tricks. Turn to "Try This!" and have some fun.
- "What's Your Opinion?" lets you say what makes people beautiful.

## Guiding Learning

### Before Reading

Read the title to students and help them understand the concept of perspective. Ask, *What does "Beauty is in the eye of the beholder" mean?* Give students some time to explore their ideas.

### During Reading

Key text to guide:

**Pages 4–5:** Ask, *Why do most people consider sight to be the most important sense?* Have students read these pages and then respond to the question. Alert students to the "Eye-Q" question. Tell them that similar questions are scattered throughout the book. As they read each question, they can check their answers on page 30.

**Pages 6–7:** Share read pages 6 and 7. Turn to the diagram and help students understand how the eye works.

**Pages 8–13:** Say, *Read to the end of page 11 and find out about some problems associated with eyesight and how technology is being used to help.* When students have finished, discuss these problems and the time line on page 11. Read pages 12 and 13 to students. Challenge them to state why Helen Keller was special.

**Pages 14–19:** Have students read these pages independently. (Share read with students needing support.) Then talk about the effects of perspective in interpreting what we see.

**Pages 20–23:** Ask, *Is seeing always believing?* Have students discuss examples of illusions, and then read to the end of page 23. Invite students to discuss the eye tricks and what they saw.

**Pages 24–27:** Talk about the importance of experience and point of view in influencing how the brain interprets visual events. Then have students read these pages and comment. Reread page 27 with students. Encourage them to identify any stereotypes they may hold, especially in terms of gender and age. Challenge students to discuss the validity of these.

**Pages 28–29:** Have students read these pages independently. Help them understand how beliefs change over time and are affected by many social and political issues.

### After Reading

Responding: Invite students to rank the five senses in terms of their value. Have students debate and justify their responses.

## Thinking Activity Master 17
### Eye Glossary: Locating, Checking, and Organizing Information

Tell students they are going to create their own glossary about the eye. With the students, read through the instructions on the Thinking Activity worksheet. Make time for students to compare their results.

## www.rigbyinfoquest.com
### Zone: Plants & Animals
### Link: Animal Eyes

Students can research answers on the site:

1. What does it mean when someone has "eagle eyes"?
2. What is binocular and monocular vision?
3. What can insects see?
4. What are compound eyes?
5. How can animals see in the dark?
6. How are some animals' eyes special?

### Learning Activities

Students can complete activities on the site:

- Take a look at a city from a bird's perspective.
- Match the animals to the clues.

SITESEEING · PLANTS & ANIMALS ·

What does it mean when someone has "eagle eyes"? Visit www.rigbyinfoquest.com for more about ANIMAL EYES.

# Eye Glossary

Name _____ Date _____

1. List all the words below in alphabetical order.
2. Use pages 6–9 of *Shifting Perspectives* to write a definition for each word.
3. Look up and record a dictionary's definition for each word.

| lashes | socket | retina | optic nerve | cornea |
| vision | blindness | color blindness | pupil | nearsighted |
| iris | rods | | | |

| Word | My Definition | A Dictionary's Definition |
| --- | --- | --- |
|  |  |  |

# Nonfiction Assessment Record

**Book Title:** *Shifting Perspectives*

Student _____     Date _____

| | |
|---|---|
| Say, *Read pages 6 through 9 silently.* Ask, *What are the steps involved in light reaching the retina?* | Was the student able to accurately sequence the main steps? (Critical Thinking 1) ☐ |
| Ask, *What is nearsighted vision, and what causes it?* | Was the student able to give a definition and cause? (Learning Outcome 1) ☐ |
| Say, *Read pages 10 and 11 silently.* Ask, *What was the main problem with the first contact lenses?* | Was the student able to locate the appropriate information on page 11? (Purpose for Reading 1) ☐ |
| Say, *Read pages 12 and 13 silently.* Ask, *What was special about Helen Keller's accomplishments?* | Was the student able to form an appropriate generalization? (Learning Outcome 2) ☐ |
| Say, *Read pages 16 and 17 silently.* Ask, *How does perspective change our interpretation of what we see?* | Did the student understand the significance of physical point of view, or reference? (Learning Outcome 3) ☐ |
| Say, *Read pages 20 and 21 silently.* Ask, *Why do our eyes sometimes seem to play tricks on us?* | Did the student indicate the role of the brain in trying to make sense of what is perceived? (Purpose for Reading 2) ☐ |
| Say, *Read pages 26 and 27 silently.* Ask, *What stereotypes do you think you've believed? Are they fair? Why/Why not?* | Was the student able to form and justify an opinion about stereotypes? (Critical Thinking 2) ☐ |
| Say, *Read pages 28 and 29 silently.* Ask, *What are some of the reasons people see things differently?* | Was the student able to specify at least two different reasons? (Purpose for Reading 3) ☐ |

# Student Book Notes—*The Invisible World*

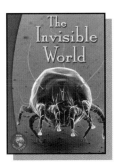

## Synopsis

*The Invisible World* explores the development and use of microscopes and other forms of technology in order to see increasingly smaller objects. The book highlights the discovery of DNA and the work of forensic scientists in solving crimes.

**Vocabulary Development**
*contaminate, electron, forensic scientist, genome, microorganism, property, protein, replicate, revolutionize, RNA, specimen*

**Challenges in the Text**
technical language

**Cross-Curricular Connections**
life science; technology; health

## Learning Outcomes

Students will:
1. recall at least two different uses of the microscope.
2. be able to explain the function of the microchip.
3. discuss possible benefits of nanotechnology.

## For Independent Readers

Provide these questions before students read the text:
- Why are some previously unsolved crimes now being solved?
- What do forensic scientists do?
- How was the microscope invented?
- How do viruses cause damage?

## Visual Elements

Students have the opportunity to:
1. read sequenced diagrams with captions.
2. view double-page spreads.
3. view a cutaway diagram.
4. view images under a microscope.

## Purposes for Reading

Possible choices include:
1. to learn how modern microscopes work.
2. to learn about the structure and function of DNA.
3. to learn about the main features of bacteria and viruses.

## Critical Thinking

Students have the opportunity to:
1. form and justify an opinion about genetic research.
2. summarize the main techniques used by forensic scientists.
3. compose and sequence information about an imaginary crime scene.

## Special Features

- Who was the first person to use a microscope? Read "Profile" and find out.
- "What's Your Opinion?" lets you have your say about gene therapy.
- What is the human code? "In the News" has the answer.
- Read "In Focus" and find out what artificial red blood cells can do.

## Guiding Learning

### Before Reading

Have students view the title page. Ask, *What is happening in the illustration? Do you think these creatures could be real?* Give time for responses.

### During Reading

Key text to guide:

**Pages 4–7:** Ask, *What have microscopes enabled us to do?* Have students read these pages independently. Then reread page 7 together. Help students understand how electron microscopes work.

**Pages 8–11:** Read these pages to students. Discuss what DNA is and what it does. Explain the diagram along the bottom of pages 8 and 9. Invite students to discuss and offer opinions on the merits of gene therapy.

**Pages 12–15:** Discuss the role of forensic scientists and some of the procedures they employ. Then have students read to the end of page 15. Discuss the way the case progressed. Highlight the importance of not making assumptions while considering all the evidence.

**Pages 16–19:** Say, *Read to the end of page 19. Find out what bacteria and viruses are and how they are similar and different.* (Share read with students needing support.) When students have finished, discuss the similarities and differences. Ensure understanding of the diagram on page 18.

**Pages 20–21:** Have students read these pages independently. Ask, *Would we be better off without mites?* Encourage students to refer to the text as they answer the question.

**Pages 22–23:** Read each of the questions to students. Have them suggest answers before reading the text.

**Pages 24–27:** Ask, *How has the invention of the microchip changed people's lives?* Give students a chance to discuss this, and then read to the end of page 27. Discuss some of the advances made in microchip technology. Highlight some of the possible uses, especially in medicine, of nanotechnology.

**Pages 28–29:** Ask, *How are clothes made of wool, cotton, and nylon different?* Have students read these pages independently and compare the uses of the different fibers.

### After Reading

Responding: Challenge students to discuss the benefits of miniaturization in medicine, computers, and communications.

## Thinking Activity Master 18

### A Schoolroom Mystery: Composing and Sequencing Information

Reread pages 12 through 15 with students and discuss the different forensic techniques used. Tell students they are going to use what they've read to create and solve their own crime. Together, read through the instructions on the worksheet before students complete the activity.

## www.rigbyinfoquest.com

**Zone: Science & Technology**
**Link: The Invisible World**

Students can research answers on the site:

1. What is genetic engineering?
2. What is pollen's appearance under a microscope?
3. Why is fossilized pollen important?
4. What is the study of microorganisms called?
5. How are microorganisms used to bake bread?

### Learning Activities

Students can complete activities on the site:

- Write your own crime-scene report.
- Design a nanorobot and explain how it works.

SITESEEING · SCIENCE & TECHNOLOGY

**What is genetic engineering?**
Visit www.rigbyinfoquest.com
for more about THE INVISIBLE WORLD.

# A Schoolroom Mystery

Name _____    Date _____

Use what you've read to invent a mystery or crime that could take place in the classroom. Describe the crime, the evidence found, and who appear to be the suspects. Perform several appropriate forensic tests, and comment on what you have found. Then use the forensic evidence to crack the case and decide on a suitable outcome.

The crime: _____

_____

_____

The evidence found: _____

_____

_____

_____

The possible suspects: _____

_____

Forensic test results: _____

_____

_____

Solving the crime (who did it and how I know): _____

_____

_____

_____

Outcome: _____

_____

# Nonfiction Assessment Record

**Book Title:** *The Invisible World*

Student _____     Date _____

| | |
|---|---|
| Say, *Read pages 4 through 7 silently.* Ask, *Can you tell me at least two different uses of microscopes?* | Was the student able to specify at least two different uses? (Learning Outcome 1) ☐ |
| Ask, *How are electron microscopes different from other types of microscopes?* | Did the student display an understanding of the key difference? (Purpose for Reading 1) ☐ |
| Say, *Read pages 8 through 11 silently.* Ask, *What is the main function of DNA in our cells?* | Did the student indicate an understanding of the role of DNA? (Purpose for Reading 2) ☐ |
| Ask, *Do you think gene therapy is a good idea? Why/Why not?* | Was the student able to form and justify an opinion? (Critical Thinking 1) ☐ |
| Say, *Read pages 12 through 15 silently.* Ask, *What are the main techniques used by forensic scientists?* | Was the student able to summarize the main techniques? (Critical Thinking 2) ☐ |
| Say, *Read pages 18 and 19 silently.* Ask, *How do viruses manage to live in our bodies?* | Did the student understand the function of a host cell? (Purpose for Reading 3) ☐ |
| Say, *Read pages 24 through 27 silently.* Ask, *What are the two main functions of microchips?* | Did the student say "processing and storing information"? (Learning Outcome 2) ☐ |
| Ask, *What are some possible benefits of nanotechnology?* | Was the student able to specify at least two different benefits? (Learning Outcome 3) ☐ |

# Student Book Notes—*The Weather Engine*

### Synopsis

*The Weather Engine* explores some of the many factors that cause the weather. It includes sections about world climate zones and the Earth's atmosphere. The book highlights the use of weather maps and how forecasters gather the information they need.

### Vocabulary Development

*altitude, computer modeling system, condense, deflect, evaporate, geostationary, humidity, meteorologist, ozone, ultraviolet radiation, water vapor, windchill factor*

### Challenges in the Text

range of maps; technical language

### Cross-Curricular Connections

earth science; technology; ecology

## Learning Outcomes

Students will:

1. display an understanding of the different climate zones.
2. be able to describe the effects of an El Niño weather condition.
3. explain the main techniques used by weather forecasters.

## For Independent Readers

Provide these questions before students read the text:

- How does the sun determine weather?
- Do all countries have four seasons?
- How do weather forecasters predict?
- What causes hail?

## Visual Elements

Students have the opportunity to:

1. view captioned illustrations.
2. read maps with keys and labels.
3. interpret a range of photographs and illustrations.
4. read text in thought bubbles.

## Purposes for Reading

Possible choices include:

1. to learn about some factors that affect the weather.
2. to learn more about the layers in the Earth's atmosphere.
3. to learn about high and low pressure systems.

## Critical Thinking

Students have the opportunity to:

1. interpret a weather map.
2. form and justify opinions about the causes of global warming.
3. gather, record, display, and analyze information about the weather.

## Special Features

- Why are some places hotter than others? Experiment with "Try This!"
- Read "My Diary" and find out who was really "stuck in the doldrums."
- Can it really rain frogs? Check out "In Focus" for the surprising answer.
- Read "What's Your Opinion?" and have your say about global warming.

## Guiding Learning

### Before Reading

Read the title to students. Ask, *What causes the weather? Why is weather different in different parts of the world?* Record these responses for the "After Reading" session.

### During Reading

Key text to guide:

**Pages 4–5:** Read these pages to students. Help students use the map and key to find particular regions. Ask, *What is the main difference between tropical and subtropical zones?*

**Pages 6–9:** Say, *How do the sun and Earth's atmosphere affect our weather?* Have students read independently to the end of page 9. First discuss the importance of the sun and then the different layers of the Earth's atmosphere.

**Pages 10–11:** Share read these pages. Highlight the dangers associated with the windchill factor.

**Pages 12–13:** Have students read these pages independently. Review the two wind maps. Challenge students to state the differences in the two weather patterns.

**Pages 14–17:** Ask, *What are high and low pressure areas?* Give students time to respond. Then have them read to the end of page 17 and comment.

**Pages 18–21:** Say, *Read to the end of page 21 to find out both how different forms of precipitation occur and how the shape of the land affects the weather.* Help students understand the differences among snow, ice crystals, and hailstones.

**Pages 22–23:** Read these pages to students. Discuss the air movement diagram, and then encourage students to use the map and key to make statements about the weather.

**Pages 24–25:** Say, *Read pages 24 and 25 to find out how people forecast the weather.* Remind students to continue to use the glossary as appropriate.

**Pages 26–29:** Have students read these pages independently. Then reread page 27 to students. Challenge each of them to form and justify an opinion on global warming. Have students talk about some of the reasons for spectacular weather phenomena.

### After Reading

Responding: Review the answers posed to the questions in the "Before Reading" session. Challenge students to amend their responses based on what they now know.

## Thinking Activity Master 19

### How's the Weather? Gathering, Recording, Displaying, and Analyzing Information

Have students gather information about temperature and precipitation. This is to be recorded on the bar graphs. Then have students use the graphs to answer the questions.

## www.rigbyinfoquest.com

### Zone: Water, Earth, & Sky
### Link: Climate

Students can research answers on the site:

1. What damage can droughts cause?
2. How does fog form?
3. What is a hoar frost?
4. How can volcanoes make the climate cooler?
5. How can scientists study past climates?

### Learning Activities

Students can complete activities on the site:

- Create your own weather map and write a weather report.
- Write an article about an extreme weather condition.

SITESEEING • WATER, EARTH, & SKY •

What damage can droughts cause?
Visit www.rigbyinfoquest.com
for more about CLIMATE.

# How's the Weather?

Name _____ Date _____

Gather and make notes about your local weather. Record the information as bar graphs. Then use the information to answer the questions.

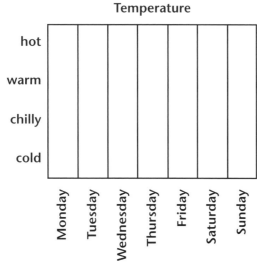

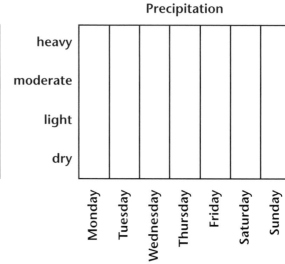

1. Which was the hottest day(s)? _____

2. What was the average temperature?_____

3. Which was the driest day(s)? _____

4. What was the average precipitation? _____

5. Considering both graphs, which were the best and worst days? Why?

_____

_____

_____

_____

_____

# Nonfiction Assessment Record

**Book Title:** *The Weather Engine*

Student _____     Date _____

| | |
|---|---|
| Say, *Read pages 4 and 5 silently.* Ask, *How are the temperate and subtropical climate zones different?* | Was the student able to use the map information to answer the question? (Learning Outcome 1) ☐ |
| Say, *Read pages 8 and 9 silently.* Ask, *Where in the Earth's atmosphere does most weather take place?* | Did the student say "troposphere"? (Purpose for Reading 2) ☐ |
| Say, *Read pages 12 and 13 silently.* Ask, *What happens during El Niño weather conditions?* | Was the student able to specify at least two appropriate weather conditions? (Learning Outcome 2) ☐ |
| Say, *Read pages 14 and 15 silently.* Ask, *What kind of conditions usually exist in a high pressure system?* | Did the student mention "clear" and "sunny"? (Purpose for Reading 3) ☐ |
| Say, *Look at the map on page 23.* Ask, *Can you describe the weather between the high and low pressure systems?* | Was the student able to use the map to indicate "cloudy" or "partly cloudy" weather? (Critical Thinking 1) ☐ |
| Say, *Read pages 24 and 25 silently.* Ask, *How do computer modeling systems help weather forecasters?* | Did the student understand that the computer generates a map? (Learning Outcome 3) ☐ |
| Say, *Read pages 26 to 27 silently.* Ask, *Should we be concerned about global warming? Why/Why not?* | Was the student able to form and justify an opinion about global warming? (Critical Thinking 2) ☐ |
| Ask, *What are three factors that affect the Earth's weather?* | Was the student able to recall at least three factors? (Purpose for Reading 1) ☐ |

© 2004 RIGBY—RIGBY INFOQUEST

# Student Book Notes—*Tides of Change*

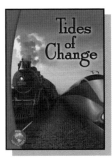

## Synopsis

*Tides of Change* traces technological advances in science, transportation, communication, and medicine over the last 200 years. Included are some of the effects these advances have had on increasing world population and dwindling resources.

## Vocabulary Development

*developed countries, developing countries, general cargo, inorganic, life expectancy, obsolete, reclaim, renewable resources*

**Challenges in the Text**
different types of maps and graphs

**Cross-Curricular Connections**
social studies; technology

## Learning Outcomes

Students will:

1. display an understanding of a world population map.
2. be able to state some effects of the growth in global travel.
3. recall some problems associated with the use of fossil fuels.

## For Independent Readers

Provide these questions before students read the text:

- Why is the world's population increasing?
- What have been the most significant changes in travel over the past 200 years?
- How have computers changed your life?
- What may be the next great technological advance?

## Visual Elements

Students have the opportunity to:

1. read and interpret a variety of maps and graphs.
2. view a sequential diagram.
3. view a range of photographs and illustrations.

## Purposes for Reading

Possible choices include:

1. to learn about some issues surrounding population growth.
2. to learn more about transportation and trade around the world.
3. to learn about some of the changes brought about through technology.

## Critical Thinking

Students have the opportunity to:

1. summarize the benefits and problems associated with alternative fuels.
2. form generalizations from information presented in graphs.
3. form and justify opinions on a range of global issues.

## Special Features

- "Time Link" explains the popularity of camels for ancient traders.
- How are cities designed? Read "In Focus" and discover something unique.
- What is artificial intelligence? "Techtalk" has the answer.
- "What's Your Opinion?" invites your thoughts about advances in technology.

## Guiding Learning
### Before Reading
Ask, *How has technology changed your lives? How is life different than when your parents were your age?* Give students time to discuss their responses.

### During Reading
Key text to guide:

**Pages 4–5:** Read these pages to students. Discuss some of the advances made in transportation, communication, and medicine.

**Pages 6–7:** Ask, *How do natural changes to the land affect people?* Have students read these pages independently. Talk about the constant nature of change and people's attempts to reshape or reclaim land.

**Pages 8–13:** Have students independently read the body text on these pages. Then lead students to interpret the map on page 8. Ask, *Which areas of the world are the most populated?* Turn to the graph on page 13. Ask, *How are the situations in Asia and Europe different?* Talk about the usefulness of maps and graphs in presenting comparisons or relationships.

**Pages 14–17:** Ask, *Why do countries trade goods, and how have changes in transportation made a difference?* Have students read these pages independently and discuss their responses.

**Pages 18–19:** Have students read these pages independently. Then have them reread the "What's Your Opinion?" section, and invite them to justify an opinion on this topic.

**Pages 20–21:** Ask, *What are some of the problems associated with fossil fuels?* Have students read these pages, and discuss the relative merits of alternative fuels.

**Pages 22–23:** Read these pages to students. Ask, *Why do you think the plan for Canberra was such a success?*

**Pages 24–27:** Ask, *How has technology changed the ways people live?* Have students respond and then read to the end of page 27. Discuss some of these changes.

**Pages 28–29:** Read the body text to students. Then have them read the opinions of the five children and comment.

### After Reading
Responding: Invite students to choose one high-tech item in their lives and talk about why it is important to them, adding what life would be like without it.

## Thinking Activity Master 20
### What's Your Opinion? Forming and Justifying Opinions
Reread pages 28 and 29 with students. Talk about how each opinion includes a justification. Read through the Thinking Activity worksheet, ensuring students understand the task and the issues included. Then have students complete the activity. (It may be appropriate for some students to work in pairs or as a large group.)

## www.rigbyinfoquest.com
**Zone: People & Places**
**Link: Population**
Students can research answers on the site:
1. How is population measured?
2. What is an "aging population"?
3. Why are there more people on some continents?
4. What is a national census?
5. Is the world shrinking?
6. How have new telecommunications "shrunk" the world?

### Learning Activities
Students can complete activities on the site:
- Interview a classmate about moving to another country.
- Plan and build a city.

What is an "aging population"?
Visit www.rigbyinfoquest.com
for more about POPULATION.

# What's Your Opinion?

Name _____     Date _____

Think about each of the issues below. Find information in *Tides of Change.* Then write your opinion about each issue and the reasons supporting your opinion.

| Issue | Opinion | Reasons |
|---|---|---|
| **Life Expectancy** Is it a good idea to have people living longer lives? | | |
| **Sharing Resources** Should rich countries share their resources with poorer countries? | | |
| **Genetically Engineered Food** Should farmers grow genetically engineered food? | | |
| **Plastic Packaging** Is the convenience of plastic packaging more important than the environment? | | |
| **Artificial Intelligence** Is artificial intelligence a good or bad idea? | | |
| **Large Cars** Should people be able to choose the size of car they drive? | | |

THINKING ACTIVITY MASTER 20: FORMING AND JUSTIFYING OPINIONS—*TIDES OF CHANGE*

# Nonfiction Assessment Record

**Book Title:** *Tides of Change*

Student _____   Date _____

| | |
|---|---|
| Say, *Read pages 8 through 13 silently.* Say, *Look at the map on page 8. What do most people live near?* | Was the student able to interpret the map and say "water" or "ocean"? (Learning Outcome 1) ☐ |
| Ask, *What are at least two reasons why people are now living longer?* | Did the student state two different reasons? (Purpose for Reading 1) ☐ |
| Ask, *What does the graph on page 13 tell you about Asia and Africa?* | Did the student understand that there is not enough food for the population? (Critical Thinking 2) ☐ |
| Say, *Read pages 14 and 15 silently.* Ask, *What is the difference between domestic and international trade?* | Did the student display an understanding of the difference? (Purpose for Reading 2) ☐ |
| Say, *Read pages 18 and 19 silently.* Ask, *What are some benefits of faster global travel?* | Was the student able to provide at least two different benefits? (Learning Outcome 2) ☐ |
| Say, *Read pages 20 and 21 silently.* Ask, *What are the two main problems associated with fossil fuels?* | Did the student indicate pollution and sustainability? (Learning Outcome 3) ☐ |
| Say, *Choose an alternative fuel. What is one benefit and one problem with it?* | Was the student able to summarize this information? (Critical Thinking 1) ☐ |
| Say, *Read pages 24 and 25 silently.* Ask, *In what ways has digital technology changed people's lives?* | Was the student able to form an appropriate generalization? (Purpose for Reading 3) ☐ |

# Index